LIFE AFTER
BEING LAID OFF

A ROADMAP TO
REINVENTION

SAUL ERTON

ISBN: 9798867824426

Contents

Introduction..1

1 How to Cope with the Financial Stress of Being Laid Off.3

2 How to Rebuild Your Confidence After Losing Your Job
....19

3 Creating a Plan: Set Goals and Priorities.........................31

4 Updating Your Resume and LinkedIn Profile 41

5 Networking and Informational Interviews........................57

Finding the Right Job Fit 75

7 How to Ace Any Job Interview 91

8 Ways to Make Extra Money 107

9 How to Switch Careers When You Have No Relevant
Experience..123

10 Your Top Questions Answered.......................................139

Introduction

You never thought it could happen to you, but it did. The job you dedicated years of your life to is gone. Now you're left with a gaping hole in your routine, a blow to your confidence, and anxiety about what comes next. Life after being laid off can feel like wandering lost in a forest with no trail markers to guide you out. But this aimless drifting need not be your fate. There is a path forward, even if you can't see it yet. This roadmap will help you navigate the emotional upheaval, reclaim your self-worth, and emerge on the other side with a fresh vision for your career and a renewed sense of purpose. The journey won't be easy, but if you follow the signposts, you will find your way to a new beginning. A new job may come in time, but first you must rediscover yourself. Are you ready to forge a new path? The adventure starts here.

The Emotional Impact of Being Laid Off

Losing your job is one of the most difficult life events a person can experience. It's normal to feel a range of emotions - shock, denial, fear, anger, and grief. Don't bottle these feelings up. Talk to others who have been through similar situations. Let close family and friends know how they can support you. Speaking with a counselor or career coach can also help you work through challenging emotions.

- Shock and denial. Initially, you may feel stunned or unwilling to accept the news. The routine and structure of work life is suddenly gone. Give yourself time to process the change.

- Fear and anxiety. You may worry about how you'll pay bills, find a new job, or make ends meet. Try to challenge anxious thoughts and focus on the things within your control. Make a plan to review expenses and set a budget. Look into assistance programs if needed.

- Anger and resentment. Feeling upset or bitter toward your former employer is common. Find healthy ways to express anger that don't damage relationships or hurt your own wellbeing. Vent to others, engage in physical activity, or pursue hobbies that you find meaningful.

- Grief and loss. Leaving a job often means losing daily interactions with coworkers and a sense of purpose or identity. Grieving these losses is normal and important for moving on in a healthy way. Be gentle with yourself and allow the grieving process to unfold. Talking or writing about your feelings can help.

Coping with difficult emotions is challenging, but with time and effort, you can work through them. Focus on self-care, connect with your support network, and start planning your next steps. The pain will lessen, and you will build resilience to face this transition.

1 How to Cope with the Financial Stress of Being Laid Off

You thought you were safe. After years of loyal service, your company decided your position was redundant. The economy tanked and they had to cut costs, so you got laid off. Now the panic starts to set in as the reality of your financial situation becomes clear. The bills keep coming but your income has stopped. You wonder how you'll pay for essentials like rent, food, and transportation, let alone any debts you may have. The stress feels crushing as you grapple with uncertainty and financial strain.

But don't despair. There are strategies you can employ to ease the burden, take back some control of your situation, and set yourself up for future success. With planning and perseverance, you will get through this difficult time. Tighten your budget, reach out for help, and look for ways to bring in income. Have hope - you have the power to cope with your financial stress after being laid off. There are always possibilities if you open your mind to them.

Take Stock of Your Finances

The first thing you need to do is examine your financial situation. Make a list of your income sources and regular bills like rent, utilities, insurance payments, etc. Calculate your monthly income versus expenses to determine how much of a shortfall you're facing.

Once you know the specifics, you can make a realistic

budget. Look for any expenses you can reduce or eliminate, at least temporarily. Things like dining out, entertainment, and hobbies are good places to cut costs. If possible, call creditors and ask if you can lower or defer payments for a few months. Many will work with people in dire circumstances.

You should also apply for unemployment benefits as soon as possible. Although the payments likely won't match your full salary, they can help pay for essentials. Don't be too proud to accept governmental assistance programs like food assistance or Medicaid either. They exist for situations like this.

Start networking and looking for ways to earn money right away. Take on a part-time job, do freelance work in your field, drive for a ridesharing service, rent out spare rooms in your home, sell unwanted possessions online, etc. Even earning an extra few hundred dollars a month can help.

The most important thing is not to panic. Make a plan and work the plan. Cut out frivolous spending, take advantage of resources available to you, bring in money wherever possible, and stay optimistic. With time and perseverance, you will get through this difficult period. Focus on the light at the end of the tunnel rather than the darkness around you. There are always alternatives and solutions if you search for them.

File for Unemployment Benefits Right Away

The first thing you should do is file for unemployment

benefits. This will provide you some income to help cover essential expenses like housing, food, and transportation while you look for a new job.

To qualify for unemployment, you must have lost your job through no fault of your own. You will need information like your Social Security number, your former employer's details including dates of employment and wages earned. The process typically takes around 30 minutes to complete. Most states allow you to file online, by phone, or in person.

While unemployment benefits are not a long-term solution, they can help relieve some of the financial stress. The average benefit nationwide is around $300-$500 per week. However, the total amount and duration of benefits depends on factors like your past wages and the unemployment rate in your state.

Some other options to explore:

- Apply for assistance programs like food stamps or Medicaid to help cover essential costs.
- Look into severance pay from your former employer. Some companies provide a lump sum payment or continue paying wages for a period of time.
- Ask creditors about hardship forbearance programs to temporarily lower or postpone payments. Interest charges are often suspended during forbearance.
- Reduce or eliminate unnecessary expenses. Go over your budget line by line and cut out things like dining out, entertainment, and hobbies. Lower utility

usage and see if you can reduce or eliminate subscription services.

- Consider taking on part-time work or freelancing to generate extra income. Every little bit helps when money is tight.

While the financial stress of job loss can seem overwhelming, there are resources and options available to help you through this difficult transition period. Stay positive—with time and persistence, you will get back on your feet.

Cut Unnecessary Expenses

Cutting unnecessary expenses is one of the best ways to relieve financial stress after losing your job. Look for costs you can reduce or eliminate to free up money for essentials like housing, food, and transportation.

Cancel unused subscriptions

Do a quick review of monthly subscriptions and services you pay for like streaming music, video, news, gaming platforms, box deliveries, etc. Ask yourself which you really use and value, then cancel the rest. Those $5 to $20 per month charges add up fast and cutting them can save hundreds per year.

Reduce utility bills

Little changes can lower your utility costs significantly. Turn the thermostat up a few degrees in summer or down in winter, use fans instead of air conditioning when possible, turn off lights/electronics when leaving a room, limit use of large appliances during peak rate periods.

Cut the cord

If you have cable or satellite TV service, canceling it can save $50 to $150 per month. With so many low-cost streaming options today, you likely won't miss it. You can always re-subscribe once your situation improves.

Buy generic or in bulk

Opt for cheaper generic or store brand items over name brands. Stock up on non-perishables you use regularly when they're on sale. Shop less frequently to avoid impulse purchases. Buying in larger sizes or quantities often lowers the unit price, saving you money in the long run.

Make meals at home

cooking meals at home versus dining out or getting takeout is one of the biggest money savers. Aim for making meals at home 5-7 times per week. Limit more expensive ingredients and stick to sales on staples like rice, beans, chicken, and veggies. Cooking in bulk on the weekends and freezing portions for the week ahead saves time and money.

With determination, you can find ways to cut $500 to $1,000 per month or more in discretionary spending through a combination of these and other cost-saving measures. While it may require adjustments, reducing expenses will help ensure you can pay for essentials during this challenging financial time. Staying focused on what really matters --

your necessities, health, relationships, and wellbeing -- can help lessen the stress. This difficult period will pass.

Look for Other Sources of Income

The loss of income from being laid off can be devastating. While you're searching for new work, tap into other sources of money to help pay the bills.

Look into unemployment benefits

File for unemployment as soon as possible. The funds can tide you over for a few months as you pursue new work opportunities. The amount you receive will depend on factors like your previous salary and location. Although the benefits likely won't replace your full paycheck, every bit helps during this difficult time.

Explore side hustles

A side gig is a great way to generate extra money in a pinch. Think about skills you have that you can monetize like freelancing, driving for a ridesharing service, walking dogs, selling unwanted items online, or driving for a food delivery app. The key is to find something flexible that works with your schedule so you can continue your job search. Any amount earned from a side hustle can help offset living expenses. More on this later.

Ask friends or family for loans

Don't be afraid to ask close ones for financial help. Explain your situation honestly and request either a short-term loan or for them to temporarily cover certain bills like groceries, utilities or rent. Offer to sign an IOU or repayment plan to make the arrangement feel more formal and help avoid hurt feelings or damaged relationships down the road. Only borrow what you can pay back to avoid being overly indebted to others.

Look into assistance programs

Many government and non-profit programs offer aid for those facing financial hardship. See if you qualify for SNAP food stamps, Medicaid, utility bill assistance or housing subsidies. Some churches and charities also provide emergency funds and grants for those recently unemployed. Do some research on programs in your area and apply as soon as possible to avoid gaps in essential services.

The period after a layoff is difficult but temporary. Exploring all options for income and assistance will help ensure your basic needs are met until you land on your feet again with steady work. Stay positive—this stressful time will pass.

Use Your Savings Wisely

Being laid off is stressful enough without adding financial worries to the mix. Your emergency fund and any savings you have should be used judiciously now to avoid further anxiety.

Make a budget

The first step is to review your income and expenses to get a clear picture of your cash flow situation. List all sources of income like unemployment benefits, spouse's salary, investment dividends, etc. Then list essential expenses such as rent/mortgage, groceries, utilities, loan payments, etc. Look for expenses you can reduce or eliminate, at least temporarily. Having a solid budget will give you more control over your finances during this difficult time.

Once you have a budget, determine how much you need each month to cover necessary expenses. Then see how much you have in readily available savings and how long that can sustain you. Make sure to keep enough in savings for an emergency fund in case of unexpected costs like medical bills or car repairs.

Reduce non-essential spending

Now is the time to cut out discretionary purchases and only spend on essentials. Stop dining out, cancel streaming services, and avoid shopping for clothes or hobbies. Cook meals at home, utilize free entertainment like public libraries, and find low-cost hobbies to fill your time.

Look into assistance programs

Don't be afraid to ask for help. See if you qualify for unemployment benefits, food assistance, utility bill help or mortgage relief. Many charities and government programs are designed specifically for those facing financial hardship. Swallow your pride and apply as soon as possible.

Using your savings and reducing spending during this

transitional time will help ensure you have enough to cover necessities until you find a new job or source of income. Staying financially stable will reduce stress so you can focus your energy on moving forward in a positive way.

Negotiate With Creditors

When times are tough financially after a layoff, negotiating with creditors may be necessary to avoid defaulting on payments or damaging your credit. It's a stressful situation but staying proactive can help set you up for success down the road.

First, gather details on all your accounts - loans, credit cards, utilities, insurance, cell phone, cable, etc. Note interest rates, minimum payments, and balances for each. See where you can trim the fat or reduce payments. Lowering cell phone data, eliminating cable, or dropping insurance coverage you don't need can free up funds to put towards more important bills.

Next, call creditors for cards and loans to request an APR reduction, temporary payment reduction or suspension, or alternative repayment plan. Explain your situation honestly and ask if they offer assistance for those facing financial hardship. Many creditors work with customers, especially if you've been timely in the past. They may lower rates, waive fees, or allow smaller payments for 3-6 months.

For secured debts like a mortgage, contact your lender to inquire about options such as forbearance, loan modification, or refinancing. Explain you intend to resolve the situation but need temporary relief. Provide details on your income loss and efforts to replace it. Ask if they offer unemployment mortgage assistance or disaster forbearance programs. The key is open communication and a willingness to provide any documentation requested.

Don't stop with phone calls. Follow up in writing via email or letters. Reiterate your requests and reaffirm your commitment to resolving the obligations. The paper trail can help if disputes arise later. Also, check credit report sites weekly to ensure your accounts are being reported properly during this time.

While negotiating with creditors is difficult, maintaining open and honest communication is key. Explain your circumstances, provide details to support requests for relief, and follow up regularly in writing. With time and perseverance, you can come to agreements that prevent further financial stress. Staying determined and proactively working with creditors will help establish footing to build back from after a layoff.

Consider Healthcare Options

With the loss of your job, keeping your health insurance coverage should be a top priority. You have a few options to consider:

COBRA

The Consolidated Omnibus Budget Reconciliation Act (COBRA) allows you to temporarily extend your current health insurance for up to 18 months. You'll have to pay the full premium yourself, but it may be worth it to keep your existing coverage and doctors. The downside is that COBRA plans can be expensive.

Health Insurance Marketplace

You can shop for new health plans on your state's health insurance marketplace or exchange. Private plans and government subsidies are available depending on your income. Look for "catastrophic" or high-deductible plans if you need to keep costs down. Marketplace plans can be more affordable than COBRA, with coverage starting the first of the following month after you enroll.

Medicaid

If your income has dropped significantly, you may now qualify for Medicaid, which provides health coverage for low-income individuals including children, pregnant women, the disabled, elderly, and parents of dependent children. Eligibility and benefits vary by state. Medicaid is administered by the states and funded by both the federal government and state governments.

- Check if you qualify based on your new income and family size. Medicaid coverage is very comprehensive and affordable, with little to no cost to you.
- Apply for Medicaid as soon as possible after losing your job. Coverage can start as soon as the first day of the month that you apply.

- You may be subject to periodic reviews of your eligibility and income to maintain coverage. Report any income or family changes right away.
- If approved for Medicaid, you must disenroll from any other health plans like COBRA to avoid paying double premiums. Medicaid will become your primary insurance.

Take the time now to explore all your options and enroll in a plan that will give you continued peace of mind. Your health and financial well-being depend on it.

Lean on Your Support System

When you've lost your job, it can feel like your financial security and stability have been pulled out from under you. During this difficult time, lean on your support system for help.

Family and Friends

Call on your close ones for emotional and practical support. Let them know specifically how they can assist you, whether it's lending an ear to listen, providing job leads, or helping out financially if needed. Don't be afraid to ask for help— that's what loved ones are for.

Professional Connections

Reach out to former colleagues, managers, and mentors. They may know of job openings that match your skills and experience. Also connect with people in your industry through networking events, LinkedIn, and alumni associations. Put the word out that you're on the job market.

Community Resources

Many local organizations offer resources for those dealing with unemployment or financial hardship. Check with places of worship, nonprofit groups, and social services agencies in your area. They may provide assistance such as:

- Food and bill payment aid
- Job training programs
- Career counseling and networking events
- Temporary work opportunities
- Healthcare options

Online Support Groups

Seek out online communities of people in similar situations. Facebook groups, message boards on sites like Indeed.com and Monster.com, and unemployment subreddits on Reddit can all provide support. You can ask questions, share advice, discuss challenges, and feel less alone. These digital support groups are available 24/7.

Losing your job and source of income is difficult, but the situation is temporary. Stay determined and focused on the future by relying on all the resources and support available to help you through this challenging time. Keep your head high—a new opportunity could be just around the corner. With the help of others, you will get back on your feet again.

FAQ on Coping With the Financial Stress of Being Laid Off

With the shock of being laid off comes the harsh reality of

how you're going to pay the bills. The uncertainty can feel overwhelming. Here are some of the most frequently asked questions about coping with the financial stress of losing your job:

How do I pay for essentials like rent, food and utilities?

Focus on necessities first. See if you can reduce or temporarily stop non-essential expenses like streaming services, gym memberships or dining out. Ask if you can make payment arrangements for important bills. Don't be afraid to ask friends or family for help or look into assistance programs in your area. Making a barebones budget can help give you clarity and a sense of control.

Should I use my emergency fund?

Your emergency fund is meant for situations like this. Use it to cover essential costs as you look for your next job. Make sure to also file for unemployment benefits to have some income coming in. If your fund runs out, cut more expenses, and see if you can take on temporary or part-time work.

How do I avoid racking up debt?

Do not turn to high-interest credit cards or loans to fill the financial gap. Only spend money on absolute necessities. Look for ways to earn extra income, whether doing freelance work, driving for a ridesharing service, or participating in market research studies. Ask creditors about forbearance programs to temporarily reduce or suspend payments without penalty.

What about health insurance?

Losing your job typically means losing your employer-sponsored health benefits. Look into extending your current coverage through COBRA or enrolling in a plan on your state health insurance exchange. Medicaid may also be an option depending on your income. Make sure any medical needs are addressed before your current coverage ends to avoid paying out of pocket.

The uncertainty of unemployment can be difficult to navigate. Connecting with others in a similar position, making a plan, and taking things day by day will help reduce the stress. With time and perseverance, you will get through this challenging period.

You know how to create a budget, cut unnecessary expenses, and find additional income to keep yourself afloat during this time of transition. You understand the importance of maintaining your health insurance and taking care of your mental health. Most importantly, you recognize that this is only a temporary setback and there are more opportunities ahead. Stay focused on your goals, keep putting one foot in front of the other, and don't lose hope.

2 How to Rebuild Your Confidence After Losing Your Job

You have a wealth of experience and abilities that any company would be lucky to have. Make a list of your key skills, strengths, and accomplishments from your most recent position. Think about any major contributions you made that improved things for the business or your colleagues. These are your strengths - your secret weapons in the job market.

Some examples might be:

- Effectively managed multiple high-priority projects with tight deadlines

- Streamlined processes to increase team efficiency by over 25%

- Achieved the highest customer satisfaction ratings in the department for over a year

- Reduced costs by negotiating with vendors and suppliers

- Mentored and coached 5 new team members on best practices

Recognizing your strengths builds confidence from within. Keep this list handy for motivation and add to it as you gain new insights. When you start interviewing again, these skills and strengths will become your stories and examples to share. Speak about them with pride and enthusiasm.

You have so much talent and ability within you. Don't underestimate the value you can provide to another organization. While the job market is challenging, by focusing on your strengths you will find the right opportunity.

Staying positive and determined will help shift your mindset. You have a choice - you can view yourself as someone unemployable who was "laid off", or as a highly skilled and accomplished professional on a quest for a new challenge. How you see yourself matters most.

The skills and strengths you possess have not disappeared. Have confidence in your abilities and keep putting one foot in front of the other. Your next great job is out there waiting for you.

Update Your Resume to Reflect Your Strengths

You were let go from your job, and now your confidence has taken a hit. To rebuild it, focus on your strengths and update your resume.

Identify your key skills and major accomplishments

Think about the key skills and strengths you utilized in your role, as well as any major accomplishments or contributions you made to the company. These could include:

- Technical or software skills: Proficiency with key tools, programs, or machinery

- Soft skills: Communication, critical thinking, problem-solving, time management, etc.

- Metrics and key performance indicators: Increased sales, improved efficiency, reduced costs, high customer satisfaction, awards, or recognition, etc.

Write them all down. This will remind you of your capabilities and the value you provide.

Update your resume to prominently feature these strengths

With a list of your key skills, strengths, and accomplishments in hand, update your resume to prominently highlight them:

1. In your experience section, emphasize related responsibilities and quantifiable achievements. Use powerful and compelling language to demonstrate the impact you made.

2. Include a separate skills section with a bulleted list of your relevant technical and soft skills. Place this prominently at the top of your resume.

3. Add any awards, honors or quantifiable metrics under your experience section for each role. Numbers, percentages, and dollars are powerful.

4. Get feedback from others on how to improve your resume. Incorporate their suggestions and advice.

5. Review and practice talking about your updated resume. This will boost your confidence in discussing your experience and qualifications with potential employers.

With a resume that effectively articulates your skills, strengths, and accomplishments, you'll start to rebuild your confidence. You have so much to offer, and the right opportunity for you is out there.

Network and Connect with Others in Your Industry

Networking after losing your job is one of the best ways to rebuild your confidence and find new opportunities. Connecting with others in your industry can lead to mentorship, job openings, collaborations, and more.

Reach out to Former Coworkers

Your former coworkers understand your work experience and skills. Send a message saying you're on the job market again and would appreciate their support. Ask if they know of any job leads or would be open to providing a recommendation on LinkedIn. Even if they can't directly help, maintaining these relationships is valuable.

Explore Professional Groups

Look for local networking groups, nonprofits, or online communities in your industry. Attend events, join discussions, and connect with others who share your professional interests. Put yourself in new situations where you can promote your experience and skills. Someone may know of an opening that matches your background. At a minimum, you'll expand your network and learn new trends in your field.

Find a Mentor

A mentor can provide guidance during your job transition and help rebuild your confidence. Look for respected individuals in your industry, either former managers or new connections from networking. Explain your situation and ask if they'd be willing to mentor you. Meet regularly to discuss the job market, get advice, and brainstorm new opportunities. Their support and encouragement can help motivate you during difficult times.

Volunteer Your Skills

Volunteering is a great way to boost your confidence, learn new skills, and contribute to a good cause. Look for organizations that would benefit from your abilities and experience. Reach out and offer your time and talents. Not only will you stay active and connected to your industry, but the experience may lead to a job recommendation or open position. Helping others also gets your mind off your own worries and challenges.

Rebuilding confidence after losing a job takes conscious effort and time. While it may feel discouraging, stay focused on surrounding yourself with a strong support network. Keep putting one foot in front of the other, learn from your experiences, and new opportunities will emerge. You have so much to offer, so get out there and show the world what you're capable of.

Consider How This Opportunity Creates New Possibilities

Losing your job can be devastating and make you question your self-worth. But this unforeseen setback also presents an opportunity to rebuild your confidence from the ground up.

Consider How This Opportunity Creates New Possibilities

Take a step back and look at the bigger picture. Losing your job frees you up to pursue new avenues you never considered before. Maybe there's a passion project you've always wanted to explore, or a hobby you've wanted to turn into a side hustle. Now is the time to experiment. Starting a blog, freelancing, volunteering, taking an online course — the options are endless. Diving into something new will boost your confidence and open your mind to different career paths.

You have a chance to redefine your priorities and values. Were you truly happy in your old role? If not, use this time to determine what really matters to you in a job or career. Once you identify what motivates and fulfills you, you'll feel more empowered in your search. Don't feel pressured to rush into any new opportunity, as that may end up damaging your confidence even more if it's not the right fit.

Networking can lead to unexpected doors opening. Start reaching out to your connections and letting them know you're on the market for new work adventures. Someone may know of an unadvertised role that suits your skills. Or a quick coffee chat could turn into a mentorship. Putting yourself out there builds confidence through social interaction and opens up unknown opportunities.

Your skills and experience have value, even if you can't see it yet. Make a list of your key strengths, accomplishments, and quantifiable wins from your most recent role. Then translate how those skills could benefit another company or in a different field. This exercise helps combat feelings of inadequacy and gives you solid proof points to share with potential new employers. With time and persistence, your confidence will be restored and you'll gain a new appreciation for your abilities.

Staying positive and proactive is the key to success. While the days may feel long, keep putting one foot in front of the other. Maintain a routine, limit negative self-talk, and focus on small acts of progress each day. Don't dwell on what you lost, but rather what you stand to gain. Your confidence may have taken a hit, but with work you will build it back, perhaps stronger than before. This temporary setback will soon be seen as the pivotal point that led you to bigger and better opportunities.

Practice Self-Care and Positive Affirmations

To build your confidence after losing your job, self-care and positive self-talk are essential. Make time each day to recharge and reconnect with the amazing person you are.

Practice Daily Self-Care

Give yourself at least 30 minutes a day to do something you enjoy. Read a book, take a walk outside, cook a healthy meal, call a friend, or engage in light exercise like yoga. When you make self-care a priority, your mood and motivation will improve. You'll gain a more balanced and optimistic perspective to help move forward in your job search.

Challenge Negative Thoughts

It's normal to have moments of self-doubt after losing your job. But don't let negative thoughts hold you back. Notice negative thoughts about your abilities or worth and reframe them into more constructive ones. For example, change "I'm not good enough to get a new job" to "This is a chance for me to find an even better job match." Speak to yourself with encouragement and praise, as you would a close friend.

Practice Daily Affirmations

Affirmations are positive statements you repeat to yourself to build confidence from the inside out. Come up with a list of affirmations that resonate with you, such as:

- I have valuable skills and experience.

- New opportunities are ahead for me.

- I am resilient and will succeed.

Repeat your affirmations while looking at yourself in the mirror. This helps to strengthen their impact. Refer to your list whenever you start to feel discouraged. Affirmations work best when you practice them daily with an open and willing attitude.

Connect with Your Support Network

Don't isolate yourself during this transition period. Call on close family and friends who lift you up and inspire you. Let them know how they can offer support. Whether it's helping review your resume, providing job leads, or just lending an understanding ear, your support network can help motivate and encourage you. Their belief in you will help fuel your own self-belief.

Set Small, Achievable Goals to Rebuild Momentum

Getting laid off can shake your confidence to the core. When your job is such a big part of your identity and daily routine, losing it leaves you feeling adrift and insecure about your abilities. The best way to rebuild confidence is through action - by setting small, achievable goals and tasks to accomplish each day. Start with baby steps to build momentum and a sense of progress.

Make a list of 3 to 5 straightforward things you want to get done each day, like:

- Update your resume. Focus on one section or bullet point at a time.

- Research new career options. Spend 30 minutes exploring job sites or professional networks.
- Connect with former colleagues. Message one person per day to say hello and share your news. Let them know you're on the market for new opportunities.
- Learn a new skill. Take an online course for just 15 or 20 minutes a day. Over time, you'll build up your knowledge and have a new accomplishment to add to your resume.
- Exercise. Go for a walk or do an at-home workout. Exercise releases feel-good endorphins that boost your mood and confidence.
- Tackle household chores or errands. Small tasks that provide a sense of productivity and control over your day.
- Make progress on a hobby project. Do something creative that sparks your passion and motivation.
- Eat healthy and hydrate. Take good care of yourself by maintaining a proper diet and drinking plenty of water. Your physical health impacts your mindset and outlook.
- Review your list at the end of each day and acknowledge what you achieved. Don't be too self-critical. Celebrate each small victory along the way. Over time, these minor successes will build upon themselves, restoring your confidence and momentum to take on bigger challenges. Stay focused on your progress and maintain a positive growth mindset. Before you know it, you'll be back on track and pursuing new opportunities.

FAQ: Answering Common Questions on Rebuilding Confidence After Job Loss

Common questions often come up when rebuilding your confidence after losing a job. Here are some of the FAQs and how to overcome them:

What if I can't find another job?

It's normal to feel anxious about finding new work, but don't lose hope. Expand your search to different fields or locations. Polish your resume, work on your interview skills, and network. Something will come along if you persevere.

How do I stop doubting myself?

Self-doubt is often the result of negative self-talk. Challenge those thoughts and replace them with more constructive ones. Focus on your strengths, skills, and accomplishments. Remember, one rejection or setback does not define you. With time and practice, self-doubt will fade.

How can I stay motivated during my job search?

Set small, achievable goals to keep momentum, e.g. update your LinkedIn profile, research companies of interest, contact old colleagues or mentors. Celebrate milestones to stay motivated for the next goal. It also helps to maintain a routine, limit distractions, and do things that boost your confidence like exercising or pursuing a hobby.

How can I avoid becoming isolated?

Make an effort to connect with others. Call friends and family, volunteer, join an online community, or take a class on something you enjoy. Getting out and engaging with people will boost your mood and motivation. Don't withdraw - let your support network help and encourage you.

Rebuilding confidence is challenging but achievable by maintaining a positive mindset, focusing on self-care, and taking purposeful action. Stay patient and remember, this transition will strengthen your resilience for future life events. Answering these common questions can help alleviate concerns and guide you to becoming a happier, more self-assured person.

3 Creating a Plan: Set Goals and Priorities

Once the shock of being laid off has worn off, it's time to start planning your next steps. A key part of moving forward is researching new opportunities and tapping into your network.

Explore Job Postings

Check sites like Indeed, LinkedIn, Monster and Glassdoor for openings in your field. Make a list of potential jobs that match your skills and experience. This helps determine areas to focus your search and see what qualifications or new skills may be required.

Tap Into Your Connections

Reach out to former colleagues, bosses, mentors, and friends. Let them know your situation and ask if they know of any opportunities. Ask if they would be willing to provide a recommendation or introduction. Also connect with people in your industry through online networks like LinkedIn. Join relevant LinkedIn groups and start engaging to build new connections.

Consider Additional Training or Certification

See what current job postings are looking for. If there are certain skills, software proficiencies or credentials that could make you a stronger candidate, look into obtaining them. Take additional courses or pursue new certifications to boost your resume. The investment in yourself will pay off.

Research Companies of Interest

Make a target list of companies you're interested in. Study their websites to learn more about them, their mission and values. Follow them on social media to get a sense of their company culture. This can help determine if they may be a good fit, uncover new opportunities, and allow you to speak knowledgeably about them during an interview.

The key is to be proactive. While searching for a new job can be challenging, focusing your efforts, enhancing your skills, and tapping into the power of connections can help land you in an exciting new role. With hard work and persistence, the perfect opportunity is out there waiting for you.

Set Short-Term and Long-Term Goals

Now that you've gone through the initial shock and taken time to process this life change, it's time to start planning your next steps. The most important things you can do are set both short-term and long-term goals to work towards. These goals will help give you direction and propel you forward into this new chapter.

Short-Term Goals

In the weeks and months immediately following a layoff, focus on achievable short-term goals. Some examples could be:

- Update your resume to reflect your most recent position and accomplishments. Polish and perfect it.

- Build your professional network by connecting with former colleagues and managers on LinkedIn. Reach out and let them know your situation has changed and you're on the market for new opportunities. Ask them to keep an eye out for any jobs that match your experience.

- Research new career opportunities and paths that align with your skills and interests. Look at current job listings to see what kinds of positions are out there. You may discover an exciting new field you want to explore.

- Take additional courses or pursue training to strengthen your skillset. Use this time to learn new skills that will make you a strong candidate.

- Meet with a career coach who can help you create a tailored career action plan. They can help determine next steps and hold you accountable.

Long-Term Goals

Once you've achieved some initial short-term goals, you can start mapping out bigger long-term goals, like:

- Landing a new full-time job in your chosen field within 3 to 6 months. This may take many informational interviews, customizing your resume for different positions, and a lot of persistence. But having a target timeframe will keep you motivated.

- Making a career change to an entirely new industry within the next year. This would require going back to school for additional certifications or training, interning, and aggressively networking. A longer time period provides flexibility while still giving you a deadline to work towards.
- Starting your own business. If you have a skill, talent or service you can monetize, set a goal to launch within 12-18 months. Figure out a business plan, work on your marketing strategy, and start setting money aside to finance it. Self-employment may be a great option, especially if jobs in your previous field are scarce.
- Relocating to a new city or state for a fresh start. Sometimes a big life event like a layoff is the catalyst for an exciting new adventure in a different place. Set a goal to move within 6-12 months, giving yourself adequate time to job hunt from afar and make arrangements. A new environment can open you up to new possibilities.

The future may feel uncertain now, but by establishing concrete short-term and long-term.

Prioritize Your Physical and Mental Health

After being laid off, it's easy to let your physical and mental health slip. However, now more than ever, it's critical to make them a top priority. Your health and wellbeing directly impact your motivation, resilience, and ability to pursue new opportunities.

Make time each day for exercise like walking, yoga, or strength training. Even just 30 minutes a few times a week can help reduce stress and boost your mood. Staying active releases endorphins that improve your state of mind and encourage positive thinking.

Also prioritize sleep, aiming for 7 to 8 hours per night. Lack of sleep impairs your cognitive abilities, decision making skills, and emotional regulation. Establish a relaxing bedtime routine, avoid screens before bed, and go to sleep/wake up at the same time each day.

Watch what you eat as well. A balanced diet with plenty of nutrients will give you the energy you need. Limit excess sugar, caffeine and alcohol which can worsen symptoms of anxiety or depression. Staying properly fed and hydrated keeps your body and mind performing at their best.

Connect with others who support you. Call on close family and friends, or join an online community of others in your field or city. Let people know you're looking for work and see if they know of any opportunities. Talking to others who have been through similar experiences can help combat feelings of isolation.

Practice self-care techniques like meditation, deep breathing, journaling or mindfulness exercises. Reducing negative thoughts and managing stress increases your resilience and ability to stay motivated. Even taking short breaks to unplug and recharge will help you maintain a positive outlook.

Your physical and mental health should be a top priority

right now. Staying active, well-rested, and connected with your support network will ensure you're able to focus, adapt to changes, and pursue new opportunities with motivation and determination. Place importance on self-care and managing stress so you can think clearly and stay optimistic about the future.

Look Into Upskilling or Further Education

Once you've taken time to process being laid off and set some initial priorities, consider if further education or upskilling could benefit your job search or career pivot.

Look Into Online Courses

There are many free or low-cost online courses available on platforms like Coursera, Udemy, or LinkedIn Learning where you can build skills that could make you a strong candidate for new jobs. Some options to explore include:

- Learning a new software, tool, or technical skill that's in demand in your industry. For example, if you have experience in marketing, learn Google Ads or SEO. If you're in healthcare, explore medical coding or billing courses.

- Brushing up on soft skills like communication, critical thinking, or project management. These versatile skills are useful across many jobs and industries.

- Exploring courses in an industry or job you're interested in transitioning to. For example, if you want to move into IT, complete intro courses on web development, UX design, or data analysis. This can help you determine if the field is the right fit and builds relevant experience.

Research Going Back to School

If you want to make a bigger career change or advance your education, research programs at local colleges or universities. Some options to consider:

- Associate's or bachelor's degrees in an in-demand field. While the time and cost commitments are greater, the long-term benefits to your career can be huge.

- Professional certifications in areas like accounting, teaching, or healthcare. These are often more affordable and faster to complete than a full degree.

- Graduate programs like a master's degree, if you want to switch to a role that requires an advanced education. Some master's programs offer concentrations that can prepare you for a career change.

The most important thing is focusing your efforts on education and skills that will directly support your goals after being laid off. Do some self-assessment to determine areas of interest and strength, and look for programs that align with the job or career path you want to pursue. With time and dedication, upskilling and further education can help put you in a better position to land the right new opportunity.

Explore Alternate Career Paths and Interests

Now that you've gone through the initial shock of being laid off and taken time to process your emotions, it's time to start thinking about next steps. A key part of moving forward is exploring alternate career paths and interests. This will help open your mind to new possibilities and make sure you find fulfilling work again.

Brainstorm Your Options

Grab a notebook and pen and make a list of jobs or fields you're curious about. Think about positions you've always wondered about, or work that matches your natural talents and strengths. Some ideas to consider include:

- Consulting in your area of expertise. If you have a lot of experience, you can market your knowledge and skills to other companies.

- Teaching or training. Do you have skills or knowledge that would be useful for others to learn? Look at local schools, bootcamps, or private clients.

- Starting your own business. Getting laid off could be an opportunity to finally pursue that entrepreneurial idea you've dreamed about. Think through the details and see if self-employment could be viable.

- Learning a new skill. Now may be the perfect time to develop expertise in an area that interests you.

Take an online course to explore the field, then look for entry-level jobs to get started.

- Volunteering or interning. Gaining new experience through volunteering or interning is a great way to try out different roles, build your skills, and network. You may discover new interests and job leads.

Research Promising Options

Once you have some ideas, start researching to determine good career path options for you. Search online to find typical job responsibilities, qualifications, salary ranges, growth opportunities, and more for positions you're interested in. See what appeals to you and matches your needs. Speak to people currently in those roles to get their input on the realities of the work.

Refine and Choose Directions

After researching various choices, determine which options you want to actively pursue. Narrow down to 2 or 3 strong contenders, then dive deeper into the requirements to make them a reality. Set goals to work towards those new career paths so you can establish a fresh start. With hard work and persistence, you'll get back on track to a fulfilling career.

4 Updating Your Resume and LinkedIn Profile

That resume you haven't touched in years and the LinkedIn profile you never optimized are now your tickets to finding a new opportunity. Your knowledge, skills, and experience haven't changed, but the way you communicate them to the outside world needs to be revamped. Employers want to see that you're active and engaged, not resting on past achievements.

Once you've dusted off that resume, do the same for your LinkedIn profile. Connect with former colleagues, join relevant industry groups, and post updates to increase your visibility.

Polish your resume and LinkedIn profile to showcase not just what you've done but who you are: a dedicated, growth-oriented professional with a proven track record of success. The job market is vast and the possibilities are many. Stay optimistic, keep networking, and keep improving your personal brand. This is merely a pause in your career, not the end.

Assess Your Current Resume and LinkedIn Profile

Your resume and LinkedIn profile are your first impression to potential employers. Make sure they're putting your best foot forward.

Review your resume

Look at your current resume with a critical eye. Are the formatting, font, and layout up-to-date and appealing? Does your resume clearly and concisely convey your experience, skills, and accomplishments? If not, it's time for an overhaul. Focus on quantifying your impact and using powerful action verbs. List your experience in reverse chronological order, emphasizing relevant and transferable skills.

Revamp your LinkedIn profile

LinkedIn is one of the top ways employers find candidates, so your profile needs to make a great first impression. Choose an appropriate yet friendly photo of yourself smiling. In your headline, emphasize your key skills, qualifications, and goals. Your summary should be a few sentences highlighting your experience and career objectives. List all your relevant work experience, education, skills, and accomplishments. Join relevant LinkedIn groups to raise your visibility.

Ask others to review

Get feedback from people who know you well, like close colleagues, managers, mentors, or career coaches. Incorporate their constructive feedback into your resume and profile. They may catch things you miss and provide useful suggestions for improvement.

With an updated, compelling resume and LinkedIn profile, you'll be ready to start networking and applying for new positions with confidence. While searching for your next role, keep enhancing your profiles as you gain new experience, skills, and accomplishments. Continuous improvement will ensure you're putting your best foot forward.

Update Your Professional Summary and Headline

Your professional summary and headline are the first things people see on your LinkedIn profile and resume.

Update Your Professional Summary

This 3-4 sentence summary should capture your career goals and strengths. Mention your years of experience, areas of expertise, and career objectives. For example:

"An innovative marketing professional with over 10 years of experience. Expertise in social media marketing, content creation, and branding. Seeking a senior marketing manager role to utilize my experience and help companies improve their digital marketing strategies."

Be sure to tailor it for the types of positions you're pursuing. Update keywords and include relevant terms that match what employers are searching for.

Revise Your Headline

Your headline is a short, attention-grabbing statement that appears below your name. It should convey your key strengths, skills, and career goals. Some examples:

- 10+ Years of Digital Marketing Experience

- Award-Winning Social Media Strategist and Manager
- Senior Content Creator and Brand Storyteller

Keep your headline to about 40 characters so it is concise yet compelling. Include keywords that match your target roles. This, along with your professional summary, gives viewers a quick overview of what you have to offer.

With an updated, targeted professional summary and headline, your LinkedIn profile and resume will make a great first impression and open doors to new opportunities.

Add New Skills and Achievements

Updating your resume and LinkedIn profile after a layoff is critical. Add any new skills, certifications, or achievements you've gained recently to show you're motivated and actively improving yourself.

Update Your Resume

Double check that your resume is tailored for the types of positions you want to apply for. Focus on relevant experience, qualifications, and measurable wins that would be valuable for those roles.

Review the last few years and note any new abilities, software proficiencies, credentials, or accomplishments you've attained. For example, have you strengthened skills in data analysis, project management, coding languages or design tools that would benefit a new employer? List those prominently on your resume.

If you completed additional training, earned a new certification or degree, highlight that as well. Continuously advancing your knowledge demonstrates your drive to grow professionally.

Beef Up Your LinkedIn Profile

Your LinkedIn profile is a digital extension of your resume. Update it regularly, especially after a job loss, to keep it current and working for you.

Add details about new skills, credentials, courses, or other professional development you've gained recently. Join relevant LinkedIn groups to connect with others in your industry and engage by posting and commenting. This raises your visibility.

Update your profile headline to reflect your goals. For example, "Senior Marketing Professional Seeking New Opportunity" or "Recently Laid Off Project Manager - Open to New Roles". Be authentic about your situation, share your value proposition and convey your enthusiasm for what's next.

Update your summary statement as well. Mention your aspirations, strengths and experience that would benefit a new company. Keep your tone positive and confident.

With some focused effort, updating your resume and LinkedIn profile can help position you as a strong candidate, ready to hit the ground running in a new role. Staying active on LinkedIn keeps you connected to people and opportunities that could lead to your next position.

Emphasize Transferable Skills

When job hunting after being laid off, updating your resume and LinkedIn profile is essential. Focus on emphasizing your transferable skills—those that you can apply across jobs and industries.

Soft Skills

Highlight interpersonal skills that you've developed over your career like communication, problem-solving, adaptability, and time management. Provide examples of how you've applied these skills in your roles. For instance, "Demonstrated adaptability by quickly learning new procedures and software after departmental restructuring." These skills are useful for many jobs, so promote them prominently.

Relevant Experience

Emphasize experience and qualifications that align with your target jobs. If changing industries, focus on transferable responsibilities and achievements. For example, "Managed three direct reports and key vendor relationships, achieving a 25% cost reduction over two years through negotiation and relationship building." The management, communication and cost-saving skills are widely applicable.

Metrics and Achievements

Quantify your major accomplishments and the impact you've

made in your roles. For example, "Reduced customer complaints by 50% year over year through improved quality assurance processes." Numeric achievements help demonstrate your value to potential employers.

Keywords

Incorporate relevant keywords from the job listings that interest you. This will help you rank higher in applicant tracking systems. For instance, if jobs call for "project management" skills, be sure to highlight "project management" in your profile and provide examples.

Online Presence

Google yourself to see what information comes up, and improve your profiles. Update your LinkedIn headline and summary to reflect your goals. Showcase relevant skills, join industry groups, and build connections. An optimized online presence, along with a compelling resume, will make you a strong candidate.

With some effort updating your resume and LinkedIn profile to emphasize your transferable skills, relevant experience, key achievements, and a professional online presence, you'll be ready to start applying to new opportunities with confidence. Best of luck!

Optimize With Keywords

Once you've updated your resume, it's time to optimize your LinkedIn profile. LinkedIn is the top professional social network and an important tool for finding new job opportunities. Recruiters and hiring managers frequently search LinkedIn to find candidates, so make sure your profile is comprehensive and optimized.

Keywords

Include relevant keywords, skills, and phrases in your LinkedIn profile that match those in your updated resume. Mention the specific tools, technologies, and programs you have expertise in. Use synonyms and related terms as well to help improve your profile's searchability. For example, if you have experience in social media marketing, include phrases like "social media specialist," "social media strategist," "digital marketing," and "content marketing."

Headline

Your LinkedIn headline is one of the first things people see in your profile. Make it compelling by describing what you do professionally in an interesting way. For example, "Social Media Marketer Driving Engagement and Conversions" or "Storyteller: Creating Content to Captivate Audiences." Keep it concise at around 10 to 15 words.

Summary

In your summary section, talk about your goals and career highlights to give the reader context around your experience and expertise. Share some of your proudest accomplishments and career successes. Discuss the impact you made in your previous roles. Keep the tone positive and enthusiastic. Your summary should be 3 short paragraphs or around 50 to 70 words each.

Experience

Make sure your experience section matches your updated resume. For each role, include 3 to 4 bullet points highlighting your key responsibilities and major contributions. Use powerful and compelling language to demonstrate the impact you made. Include quantitative results and metrics when possible.

Endorsements and Recommendations

Ask former colleagues, managers, and mentors to provide recommendations and endorse your skills on LinkedIn. Their praise and positive reviews will strengthen your profile and make you a more attractive candidate. Return the favor by endorsing them as well.

Updating your LinkedIn profile in these key ways will make you much more discoverable to new job opportunities. Take the time to polish your profile and soon you'll be networking, connecting with industry professionals, and interviewing for new roles. Staying active on LinkedIn is one of the best ways to aid your job search after being laid off.

Improve Formatting and Layout

Updating your resume and LinkedIn profile after being laid off is crucial to finding new work quickly. The way information is presented on these platforms can make or break your chances of landing an interview.

Focus on Formatting

How your resume and profile *look* is just as important as what they *say*. Employers spend mere seconds reviewing candidates, so you need to grab their attention fast.

- Use clear section headings for "Experience," "Education," "Skills," etc. Make them **bold** and increase the font size slightly.

- Within each section, list your roles and responsibilities in reverse chronological order. Use parallel grammatical construction for each entry. For example, "Managed team of 10 software engineers" and "Streamlined product development cycles by 15%."

- Use bullet points to highlight key achievements and quantify your impact whenever possible. Numbers and metrics stick in readers' minds.

- Include relevant keywords in your job titles and section headings. These will make you more searchable to employers and applicant tracking systems.

- Use a simple, clean font like Arial or Calibri, size 10-12 point. Add visual interest with italics to emphasize certain words.

- Ensure even spacing between sections and balance margins so the page looks symmetrical. Add lines or boxes for a subtle graphical element.

- On LinkedIn, include a friendly professional headshot and customize your profile URL to something simple like www.linkedin.com/in/yourname. Complete all available sections to establish yourself as an authority in your industry.

Polishing the presentation of your resume and LinkedIn profile could make a difference in rejoining the workforce. Take time to ensure proper formatting, compelling language, and a layout that is attractive as well as scannable. ,

Check for Errors and Consistency

Double check your resume and LinkedIn profile for any errors or inconsistencies before sending them out. It's easy to miss small mistakes when you've been working on these documents for a while. Do a final proofread to ensure everything is accurate and aligned.

Check for typos and grammar issues

Go over both your resume and LinkedIn profile word by word to identify any typos, spelling mistakes, or grammar problems. Have a friend or family member also review to catch anything you might miss. Double check that:

- All words are spelled correctly

- Proper nouns like company names, schools, and locations are spelled properly

- Punctuation like commas, periods, apostrophes are

used correctly

- Verb tenses are consistent and uniform

- Numbers like dates, statistics, figures, and percentages are accurate

Correct any issues you find right away. These kinds of errors make a poor impression and could get your application rejected.

Ensure consistency across documents

Compare your resume and LinkedIn profile to make sure all information is consistent and aligned in terms of:

- Job titles, company names, dates employed

- Achievements, accomplishments, and quantifiable impacts

- Skills, expertise, and keywords

- Formatting like font type, section headings

You want to present a cohesive professional brand and story across platforms. Double check that nothing differs or contradicts to avoid confusion for anyone reviewing both profiles.

Get a final review

Ask a mentor or career coach to review your resume and LinkedIn profile one last time. They may notice something you've missed or have valuable feedback on how to improve. Be open to their suggestions—a fresh set of eyes can make a big difference. Once you've incorporated any recommendations, you're ready to start applying and networking with confidence, knowing your materials are polished and primed.

Staying on top of these details and aligning your resume and LinkedIn presence will help ensure you make a great first impression. With a little time and effort, you can feel assured you've optimized your chances for success. Keep at it—the right opportunity is out there!

Customize for Each Application

When you've been laid off, updating your resume and LinkedIn profile should be a top priority. Customizing each for the specific jobs you're interested in can help boost your chances of landing an interview.

Now is the time to revisit your resume and LinkedIn summary to ensure they are compelling and targeted. Scrutinize each section, from your professional summary to your work experience descriptions. For each role, emphasize responsibilities and major accomplishments that would be most relevant for your desired position. Quantify your key wins and impacts whenever possible.

For your LinkedIn profile, create an optimized headline that incorporates important keywords related to your area of work. Your summary should be a brief but compelling overview of your experience, skills, and career goals.

Include relevant skills, join relevant LinkedIn groups, and follow influencers in your industry. Ask former colleagues for recommendations highlighting your abilities and work. These help to build your credibility.

When applying to new openings, carefully review the job listing to determine what the hiring company is looking for in a candidate. Then, for each application, customize your resume and LinkedIn profile to align as closely as possible with the desired qualifications. You may need to reorganize sections, emphasize different experiences or accomplishments, or add relevant keywords. The more tailored your application is to the specific role, the more likely you are to get a call back.

Don't get discouraged if you face rejection. The job market can be competitive, especially for in-demand positions. Stay active on LinkedIn, continue networking, and keep applying to new opportunities. With time and persistence, the right match for your skills and experience will emerge. Updating your resume and LinkedIn profile for each application is key to standing out in a sea of candidates. Keep putting in the effort, and the reward of a new job offer will be within your reach.

Leverage Your Network on LinkedIn

Now that you've brushed up your resume, it's time to turn your attention to LinkedIn. As the world's largest professional network with over 600 million members, LinkedIn is one of the top places recruiters search for candidates. Make sure your LinkedIn profile is optimized to increase your visibility and connect you with new opportunities.

First, update your LinkedIn headline to reflect your current job search status. Something like "Recently Laid Off [Your Profession] Seeking New Opportunity" works well. This signals to your network that you're on the market.

Next, revise your profile summary to highlight your experience, skills, and career goals. Mention the types of positions you're targeting. Keep this brief, around 2 to 3 short paragraphs.

Then, review and refresh your experience section. For each role, include 3 to 4 bullet points highlighting your key accomplishments and quantifiable impacts. Use active verbs and mention any awards or promotions. Add in relevant new skills or areas of expertise you've gained.

Don't forget to update your profile photo. A professional headshot in business attire is best. Smile and make eye contact with the camera to appear friendly and engaged.

Update your skills and endorsements. Add in any new skills you've obtained. Ask former colleagues and managers to endorse you for skills they can vouch for. Return the favor and endorse them as well.

Leverage your LinkedIn connections by letting them know you're on the job market. Post an update sharing your new status and types of roles you're seeking. Ask your close contacts if they know of any opportunities. Also search for

2nd and 3rd degree connections in target companies and ask for introductions.

With an optimized LinkedIn profile and an active networking strategy, you'll increase your visibility to new employers and improve your chances of finding a new role. While searching for jobs, make LinkedIn a daily habit to connect with your network, join industry groups, follow target companies, and stay on the radar of recruiters. With time and persistence, new opportunities will emerge.

5 Networking and Informational Interviews

You know that career success doesn't come from what you know but who you know. Yet the thought of networking makes your palms sweat and your stomach churn. The small talk, the superficiality, the fear of coming across as annoying or desperate - it's enough to make you want to retreat into your cubicle. But networking doesn't have to be painful or inauthentic.

Informational interviews are a secret weapon for building real connections that lead to opportunity. When done right, informational interviews create relationships, uncover insights, and open doors. The key is approaching people with a spirit of genuine curiosity about them and their experience. People love talking about themselves and their work, so give them the opportunity. Come prepared with thoughtful questions, actively listen, and look for ways to help and add value.

Follow up and stay in touch. Before you know it, you'll have built a web of connections that will propel your career in new directions. The networking payoff comes to those who invest in people, not those who see people as vehicles for personal gain. So, take a deep breath and dive in. Opportunity awaits.

What Are Informational Interviews and Why Are They Valuable?

Informational interviews are casual meetings with professionals currently in roles you aspire to. They allow you to gain valuable insights into a career path, company, or industry.

- Build your professional network. Connecting with people in your desired field can lead to new opportunities like job openings, collaborations, or mentorships.

- Learn the realities of a role. Speaking with someone currently in your dream job can help ensure it aligns with your expectations and determine if that path is right for you. You can inquire about responsibilities, challenges, and a typical day.

- Gain advice and tips. Informational interviews provide a chance to ask questions about things like the job search process, key skills or experience needed, or how to land an interview.

- Make a good impression. Conducting an informational interview professionally demonstrates your enthusiasm and communication abilities. If a position opens up, you may be on the interviewer's radar as a strong candidate.

- Do your research. Learn as much as possible about the person and company beforehand. Come prepared with thoughtful questions that show your genuine interest in the work they do.

- Follow up appropriately. Be sure to send a thank you email or note within 24 hours reaffirming your appreciation for their time and insights.

Mention specific advice or suggestions discussed that you found particularly helpful.

Informational interviews require effort and time, but the rewards of strengthened connections, valuable advice and career clarity make it worth the investment. With an open and engaged mindset, you'll gain the information and network needed to propel your career forward.

Identify Your Target Companies and Contacts for Informational Interviews

Once you know the companies and roles you're interested in, start identifying key contacts for informational interviews. These should be people currently in a position you aspire to, or work for a target company.

Search LinkedIn

The easiest way to find potential contacts is on LinkedIn. You can filter by company, location, title, and see who's in your network or a 2nd connection. When you find good candidates, check their profiles for shared interests or connections before reaching out.

Ask for Introductions

See if anyone in your network can introduce you to contacts at target companies. An intro from a mutual connection makes people more likely to respond and meet with you.

Don't Overlook "Under the Radar" Contacts

Some of the most valuable informational interviews come from people not officially in the role you want but work closely with it, e.g., administrative assistants, project managers, etc. They often have a unique perspective into the day-to-day realities of a position.

Prepare Thoughtful Questions

Come prepared with questions that show you've researched the company and role, e.g.:

1. What do you find most challenging or rewarding about your work?

2. What key skills or experiences are most important for success in this field?

3. Do you have any advice for someone looking to break into this industry or role?

4. Are there any new or innovative trends on the horizon I should be aware of?

With some legwork, you'll be having coffee with key influencers and learning the inside scoop on your dream career in no time. The effort will pay off, so start making those connections today.

Reaching Out and Setting Up the Informational Interview

Once you have a list of potential contacts for informational interviews, it's time to start reaching out. The key is to be proactive, yet courteous and considerate in your outreach.

Do Your Research

Learn as much as you can about the person and company before contacting them. Check their LinkedIn profile, company website and social media to get a sense of their background, experience, and current role. Mention something specific you found interesting or insightful in your initial outreach to show you value their time.

Craft a Personalized Message

Send a friendly, yet professional message expressing your interest in setting up an informational interview to learn more about their experience and career path. Share a bit about yourself, your goals, and why you were interested in connecting with them. Make sure your request is polite and straightforward by briefly explaining that you're looking to learn from their experiences, not ask for a job. Keep the message concise while being personable.

Provide Options and Be Flexible

Give the person a few date and time options for a quick 30-minute call or meeting when suggesting a time to connect. Recognize that their time is valuable and be willing to work around their schedule. Offer to meet in person or via phone/video chat, whichever they prefer. Provide your contact information and let them know you appreciate any time they can spare.

Follow Up and Say Thanks

If you don't receive a response within a week or so, send a polite follow-up message re-expressing your interest and providing a few more date/time options. Once you have confirmed a time to meet, send a thank you message in advance to reiterate how much you appreciate them taking the time to speak with you. Following the informational interview, be sure to send another thank you message within 24 hours recapping what you discussed and how helpful it was in gaining valuable insights. Maintaining good communication and showing your gratitude will leave a good impression and help build new networking connections.

The key to setting up a successful informational interview is being proactively thoughtful in your outreach, considerate of the person's time, flexible in your scheduling and abundantly appreciative of their willingness to share their experience and advice with you. With the right mindset and follow through, informational interviews can lead to new mentorships, partnerships, and unforeseen opportunities.

Preparing for the Informational Interview

Informational interviews are a valuable networking tool, but only if done right. To set yourself up for success, do some prep work.

Research the person and company. Learn about their role, background, and current work. See if you have any connections in common on LinkedIn. The more you know, the better questions you can ask. This shows your interest and enthusiasm.

Prepare questions ahead of time. Come armed with thoughtful questions that show you've done your homework. Ask about their career path, daily responsibilities, advice for someone in your position, industry trends, etc. Have a list of 10-15 questions in case the conversation lulls.

Review your resume and career goals. Be ready to speak briefly about your background, experience, and career aspirations. Keep your summary under 2 minutes. The interview is about them, not you, so don't overshare. But sharing some context will help them provide relevant guidance.

Dress professionally. Even though it's an informational interview, you want to make a good first impression. For an in-person meeting, business casual or business professional attire is appropriate. For a phone or video call, dress in professional attire at minimum from the waist up. Your clothing reflects your mindset.

Bring copies of your resume. Have a few copies on hand to share in case they ask for your resume or want to pass it along to a colleague. Simple resumes, portfolios, or business cards are all appropriate for informational interviews.

Send a thank you. Within 24 hours, send a thank you email or note expressing your appreciation for their time. Mention something specific you found helpful or insightful. Let them know you value their guidance. A thoughtful thank you keeps you on their radar for any future opportunities.

Following these steps will give you confidence walking into your informational interview. Do your part to prepare, and the conversation can unfold naturally as you explore the possibilities of new connections and career advice. The rewards of informational interviews often come from the relationships built through a shared exchange. So prepare to connect.

Questions to Ask at the Informational Interview

When conducting an informational interview, come prepared with thoughtful questions that will provide insight into the industry, company, role and career path. Ask open-ended questions to start an engaging discussion, rather than yes or no questions. Some suggestions include:

What does a typical day in this role look like?

Get a feel for the daily responsibilities, priorities and objectives of the position. Discuss both routine tasks as well as more complex projects. Inquire about what the job entails during busy periods versus slower times.

What background and experience are most helpful for someone in this career?

Learn about the qualifications, knowledge, skills, talents and personality traits that would make someone successful in this line of work. See if your current strengths and interests align with what is needed for this role.

What opportunities exist for career progression?

Discover the potential career paths and advancement opportunities down the road. Ask if there are higher level roles to aspire to, such as management positions. Discuss the requirements to get promoted and how long it may take.

What do you find most challenging or rewarding about your job?

Get a balanced perspective on the pros and cons, difficulties, and benefits of the work. The challenges can prepare you for the realities of the role, while the rewards will reaffirm your interest in the career path.

What advice would you give to someone interested in this field?

Request recommendations and words of wisdom from an experienced professional in your industry of interest. Their advice and guidance can help set you up for success as you pursue work in this area.

Would you be open to allowing me to shadow you for a day?

If there is interest and availability, job shadowing is an invaluable opportunity. Seeing the role in action will provide first-hand experience into what the work entails on a daily basis. Express your appreciation for their time and willingness to host you.

Informational interviews are a chance to have sincere discussions with people currently in roles you aspire to. Come with engaging questions, actively listen to their insights and advice, then follow up to express your gratitude. Building connections and learning from others is key to navigating your career journey.

Following Up After the Informational Interview

Following up after an informational interview is crucial. It's your chance to express gratitude, reiterate your interest, and stay on the interviewer's radar.

Send a thank you email within 24 hours.

Mention specific parts of your conversation that you found particularly helpful or insightful. For example, "Thank you again for taking the time to meet with me. Our discussion about your career path and experiences in the marketing field was extremely valuable. I appreciate you sharing your advice and perspectives." Keep this email brief but sincere.

Connect on LinkedIn.

Send an invitation to connect along with a personal note. For example, "It was a pleasure speaking with you yesterday. I'm looking forward to staying in touch on LinkedIn and continuing our conversation." Connecting on LinkedIn establishes an ongoing relationship and gives you both an easy way to stay up to date with each other's careers.

Follow up in a few weeks.

Drop your interviewer another quick email or LinkedIn message to reaffirm your interest in any opportunities they mentioned and ask if there are any updates. For example, "I hope all is well. I wanted to check in and reiterate my strong interest in any internship or entry-level positions on your marketing team. Please keep me in mind if any suitable roles open up." This follow up email shows your enthusiasm and motivation.

Stay engaged by commenting on their LinkedIn posts.

Like and comment on any updates, articles, or other posts your interviewer shares on LinkedIn. Engage with their content by asking questions or sharing your perspectives. This ongoing interaction and virtual networking helps to strengthen your new connection over time. When the right opportunity arises, your interviewer will already be familiar with you and may be more inclined to reach out.

Through prompt and thoughtful follow up, nurturing your new LinkedIn connection, and staying engaged with your interviewer's professional activities, you can build a lasting relationship that may lead to career opportunities down the road. The key is persistence and patience – keep putting in effort and the rewards will come.

Leveraging Your Network for Job Opportunities

Once you've built up your network through informational interviews, it's time to tap into those connections for job opportunities. Many jobs are filled through personal referrals before they're even advertised, so working your network is key.

Reach out to your connections

Go through your list of contacts and reach out to those you've connected with, expressing your interest in new job opportunities they may know about in your field. Let them know the type of position you're looking for, your key skills and strengths, and the kinds of companies you're interested in. Ask if they know of any openings that could be a good fit. Your contacts will likely be happy to keep an eye out for suitable jobs on your behalf or refer you to others in their network.

Ask for introductions

Don't hesitate to ask your connections for introductions to others in their network. A personal introduction from someone you both know is an excellent way to forge a new connection. Explain that you're conducting a job search and looking to expand your professional network. Most people will be willing to facilitate an introduction if they think there's potential for mutual benefit.

Follow up and express interest

When job leads or new connections emerge from your networking efforts, be sure to follow up promptly. Reach out to the person who provided the lead to express your sincere thanks for keeping you in mind. For new connections, send a message re-introducing yourself, referencing your mutual contact, and conveying your interest in getting to know them better and learning more about their work. Following up and maintaining communication with your network is essential to cultivating fruitful professional relationships.

Consider job referrals

For especially strong connections in your network, consider asking them for a direct job referral at their company or organization. A referral from a current employee carries significant weight with employers and may help boost your chances of landing an interview. However, only ask for a referral if you have a very solid, mutually beneficial connection with that person, and you are confident they can speak highly of your work and potential. A poor referral may do more harm than good.

With persistence and consistency, leveraging your networking efforts and connections can lead to valuable job opportunities. Keep nurturing your professional relationships, be specific about your goals, and the right job for you may emerge through your ever-expanding network.

Turning Informational Interviews into Job Offers

Turning your informational interviews into job offers is the ultimate goal. With the right mindset and follow through, you'll be well on your way to career success.

Express Continued Interest

Reach out and thank your contacts again for their time and insights. Let them know you're still very interested in the company and role. Ask if there are any upcoming networking events you could attend to connect with others, or if they'd be open to grabbing coffee again in the future. Staying engaged and building relationships will increase your chances of finding new opportunities.

Apply Your Learnings

Think about how you can apply what you've learned from your informational interviews. Revise your resume to better align with what the company is looking for. Develop relevant skills and experience that would make you a strong candidate for positions within the organization. The more you focus your efforts, the more likely the right job will come along at the right time.

Follow Up on Job Postings

Check the company's website and job sites regularly for new openings. Once something is posted that matches your interests, don't hesitate to reach out to your contacts and express your desire for an interview. Ask if they'd be willing to submit a recommendation on your behalf or help get your resume in front of the hiring manager. With an internal referral, you'll have a leg up on other applicants.

Be Persistent and Patient

The job search process can take time. While you should avoid being pushy, don't be afraid to periodically re-engage with your network connections to inquire about new opportunities. Let them know you remain very enthusiastic about joining their team. With continuous relationship-building and persistence, informational interviews often lead to job offers when the timing is right.

Informational Interview FAQs: Answering Common Questions

Informational interviews are a great way to learn more about a company or role you're interested in, but you likely have some questions about how they work. Here are answers to some of the most common informational interview FAQs:

How should I prepare for an informational interview?

Do your homework ahead of time. Research the individual and company so you can have an educated conversation. Prepare questions about their role, career path, company culture, and industry. Come equipped with a resume in case it's requested, but the focus should be on learning, not getting a job offer.

How long should an informational interview last?

Aim for 20 to 30 minutes. Be respectful of the interviewee's time. Let them know the expected length upfront and stick to it. If the conversation is going well, you can ask if they have time to continue for a few more minutes but avoid overstaying your welcome.

What types of questions should I ask?

Inquire about their experiences, insights, and advice. Ask open-ended questions about what they find most rewarding or challenging in their role, how they got started in their career, what education or skills are needed, trends in the industry, etc. Also ask for their opinions on resumes, networking, continuing education, work-life balance, or whatever topics would be most helpful for you.

Is an informational interview the same as a job interview?

No. An informational interview is purely for learning and networking purposes. Do not ask about current job openings or directly push for employment. Focus the discussion on building a connection, gaining valuable advice and input, and exploring options. While an informational interview could potentially lead to new opportunities down the road, go into it with the mindset of learning and relationship building, not getting a job offer.

Should I follow up after an informational interview?

Yes, following up is key. Send a thank you email within 24 hours to express your genuine appreciation for the individual's time and insights. Mention something specific you found helpful or interesting from your conversation. Let them know you would like to stay in touch and ask if it would be okay to reach out periodically with additional questions. Following up and maintaining contact is an important step in networking and relationship building.

Conclusion

You've made it this far in your career through hard work and perseverance, but now it's time to take it to the next level. Networking and informational interviews are the keys that will unlock new opportunities and open doors you never knew existed. Reach out to people in roles or companies that inspire you. Ask thoughtful questions about their journey and experience. Build new relationships and strengthen your existing network. Before you know it, a mentor may emerge, or a new career opportunity may present itself.

Finding the Right Job Fit

Finding the right job fit means identifying a position that aligns with your skills, values, interests, and priorities. It's a role that motivates and energizes you, and contributes to your overall well-being and work-life balance.

Some signs you've found the right job fit:

- You're passionate about the work and company mission. The role ignites your curiosity and desire to grow in your career.

- Your strengths, talents, and working style match the position's requirements. You feel confident in your ability to succeed and advance.

- The company culture and values resonate with you. You mesh well with the team and feel a sense of belonging.

- You're empowered and supported. There are opportunities for autonomy, input, and career progression.

- Compensation and benefits meet your needs. You feel financially and professionally valued.

- Work-life balance is promoted. Flex time, paid time off, and a manageable workload are offered.

To determine if a job is the right fit, evaluate the specifics of the role and company. Speak with others currently in that position. Ask about key duties, challenges, company culture, and work environment. Consider if the job aligns with your priorities like schedule, commute, salary, and growth opportunities. Finding fulfilling work suited to your needs and strengths leads to greater productivity, job satisfaction, and well-being. The right job fit can make all the difference in your career and life.

Know Your Values and Priorities

To find a job that truly fits, you need to determine what's most important to you. Think about your priorities, values, and what you want in life - not just now, but 5 or 10 years down the road.

Your Values and Priorities

What matters most in your life? Things like work-life balance, meaningful work, job security, creativity, helping others, constant learning, or advancement opportunities? Make a list of your top values and priorities. Then evaluate how well different jobs align with what's important to you.

Some questions to ask yourself:

1. Will this job allow me to maintain a good work-life balance with time for family, friends, hobbies, and self-care? If not, will the rewards of the job outweigh any sacrifices?

2. Does this position contribute value to society or help improve people's lives in some way? Do the

company's mission and values align with my own?

3. How stable and secure is this job? What are the opportunities for career growth and advancement over time?

4. Will I find the work interesting, engaging and intellectually stimulating? Or will I quickly become bored or unmotivated?

5. How well does this job utilize my key strengths, talents, and skills? Will I be able to develop new skills and expertise?

By thoughtfully considering these factors, you can determine which jobs will fulfill you and support what matters most in your life. The right job for you is out there - you just have to know what you're looking for.

Understand Your Strengths and Weaknesses

To find the right job fit, you need to know yourself. Analyze your strengths and weaknesses to determine the types of jobs you will succeed in.

Strengths: What Are You Good At?

Think about your natural talents, skills you've gained through experience, and things that energize you. Are you an effective communicator? Do you have a knack for problem-solving? Are you highly organized and efficient? Consider jobs that align with your key strengths. For example, if you're a "people person," look for roles involving teamwork, customer service, teaching, or counseling. Play to your strengths and you'll be more engaged and productive.

Weaknesses: What Do You Need to Improve?

Nobody's perfect, so identify areas you could strengthen to open up more career options. Maybe you need to boost your technical abilities or become more adaptable to change. Look for jobs that will push you outside your comfort zone so you can grow, but not so far outside that you'll struggle. With time and practice, you can turn weaknesses into strengths.

Values: What Really Matters to You?

Your values shape what motivates and fulfills you in a job. If work-life balance and stability are priorities, pursue jobs with regular hours and good benefits. If challenge and impact are important, look for positions with opportunities for growth and a chance to make a difference. Seek workplaces with a culture that aligns with what you care about. When your job matches your values, you'll find deeper meaning and satisfaction.

Evaluating your strengths, weaknesses, and values helps determine your "best fit" roles. Don't chase jobs just for a paycheck or job security. Find work you genuinely enjoy and excel at. You'll perform at your peak, achieve your full potential, and gain a sense of purpose and passion for your career. With self-knowledge and the right job fit, you'll shine.

Research Job Descriptions Thoroughly

When looking for the right job fit, thoroughly researching various job descriptions is key. Compare multiple listings for the same position to determine what the typical requirements and responsibilities are. Look for postings that match your experience and education level. The job description provides invaluable insight into what the role entails day-to-day.

Carefully read through each part of the job listing. Pay close attention to the:

- Job summary and key responsibilities. Make sure these align with your interests and strengths. Look for verbs like " coordinate," "oversee," "analyze" or "develop" that match your talents.

- Required and preferred qualifications. Do you meet the minimum requirements? Do you have any of the preferred qualifications that would make you a strong candidate? If not, consider gaining additional experience or education before applying.

- Details about the company culture and work environment. Look for companies with a culture that fits your work style and values. Some listings will give you a sense of the pace, flexibility, and formality of the work environment.

- Salary expectations or range. Make sure the salary would be suitable for your experience and financial needs before investing time in the application process. Don't waste time applying for jobs that won't meet your minimum salary requirements.

- Application instructions. Follow these instructions carefully to optimize your chances of being considered for an interview. Submit a tailored cover letter and resume that clearly shows how you are an excellent match for the position based on the job listing details.

Doing your homework and evaluating job listings closely will help ensure you pursue positions that are the right fit in terms of your abilities, work preferences, salary needs, and growth opportunities. Finding the right job fit is well worth the time and effort. With the right role, you'll be motivated and positioned for success. Keep researching and don't settle for a poor job fit.

Ask Insightful Questions During Interviews

The job interview is your chance to determine if the role and company culture are the right fit for you. Asking insightful questions shows your enthusiasm and desire to make an informed decision. Some key things to consider:

Company Mission and Values

What is the company mission? What are the core values? Do they align with your own principles and priorities? For example, you might ask:

- How would you describe the company culture here? What values are most important?

- What is your mission and how does this role contribute to it?

Understanding the company's purpose and priorities helps determine if it's an organization you want to dedicate your time and talents to.

Growth Opportunities

Ask about possibilities for professional development and career advancement. For example:

- What opportunities are there for growth and progression over the next few years?

- How does the company support ongoing employee education and skills training?

You want to work for a company that will invest in your growth and success.

Work-Life Balance

Inquire about work schedules, time off policies and how the company values work-life balance. For instance:

- Can you describe a typical work week for this role? How many hours do most people work?

- What is your time-off or vacation policy? How do you support employees in maintaining a good work-life balance?

Work-life balance is key to health, happiness and

productivity. Make sure their policies align with your needs.

Next Steps

Finally, ask about the interview and hiring process to determine appropriate next steps:

- What are the next steps in the interview process? When can I expect to hear from you?

- Is there anything else I can provide to help you make your decision?

Asking thoughtful questions during your interview will help ensure you find a role and company that fits you perfectly.

Consider Company Culture and Work Environment

When looking for a new job, determining how well you'll fit within a company's culture and environment is key. The work environment and company culture refer to the overall vibe of a workplace and how well your values and priorities align with it. Some things to consider:

Company Mission and Values

A company's mission and values statement reflect what they stand for and aim to achieve. See if their priorities match up with what you care about in a role. For example, if you value work-life balance, a company emphasizing "hustle" and constant overtime may not be the best fit. Look for companies with missions and values promoting things like work-life balance, employee wellbeing, diversity and inclusion, or environmental sustainability.

Workplace Vibe

The overall feel or vibe of a workplace encompasses things like dress code, work hours, communication styles, and how people interact. For example, a casual, flexible environment where people frequently collaborate may suit you well. Or perhaps you prefer a more formal workplace with clear hierarchies and individually focused work. Think about what energizes or drains you to determine a good vibe match.

Opportunities for Growth

Consider the opportunities for career growth and learning within a company. Look for companies that invest in employee education and development, offer mentorship programs, or provide opportunities for lateral moves into different roles. Stagnating in a position where you can't grow your skills won't lead to job satisfaction in the long run.

Management Style

A company's management style significantly impacts your day-to-day work experience. Look for companies with supportive managers who provide constructive feedback, encouragement and help remove roadblocks. Managers who micromanage or don't support work-life balance can quickly lead to burnout. Discuss opportunities for mentorship and how managers support career growth during your interview.

Taking time to evaluate company culture and work

environment will help ensure you find a role that motivates and fulfills you. The right job fit means you'll be happier, healthier, and better able to contribute to the organization's success. With some digging, you can find a company where you feel energized to do your best work.

Weigh Compensation and Benefits Packages

When evaluating job offers, the compensation and benefits packages are crucial factors to consider. Compare what each company is offering to determine which is the best overall fit for your needs.

Salary

Look at the base pay for the position and how it compares to the typical salary range. While money isn't everything, you want to make sure you'll be earning a fair and competitive wage. Think about your minimum requirements and ideal salary to determine if the offer meets your needs. Also consider opportunities for pay increases over time through raises, promotions, or bonuses.

Health Insurance

For many, health insurance is a top priority. Review the plans offered and the portion of the premium you'll be responsible for paying. Look at the coverage and out-of-pocket costs like deductibles and copays for things like doctor visits, hospital stays, and prescription drugs. Make sure the plan meets your healthcare needs appropriately.

Other Benefits

Additional benefits like paid time off, retirement plans, tuition reimbursement, and employee discounts are attractive perks that add value. Compare the paid vacation, sick leave, and holidays to your minimum requirements. See if the company matches any portion of your retirement contributions. Look at opportunities for career growth through training, education, and development programs. These types of benefits, while sometimes overlooked, are meaningful parts of an overall compensation package.

Evaluating all parts of the compensation and benefits offerings will help determine which opportunity is the best fit for your priorities and needs. Don't get dazzled by a high salary alone. Look at the total package to find the job that suits you best in both the short and long term. The ideal role is out there, you just have to weigh all the options carefully to find it.

Reflect on Day-to-Day Job Duties and Responsibilities

To find a job that's the right fit for you, it's important to reflect on what you want in your day-to-day work life. Think about the tasks and responsibilities that will keep you motivated and engaged.

- Do you want a job with a lot of variety or one that focuses on a particular skill set? Some jobs require wearing many hats, while others specialize in a narrow range of duties. Consider if you prefer tackling new challenges frequently or developing expertise in a specialized area.

82

- How much interaction with co-workers and customers do you want? Some jobs are more collaborative while others are more independent. Determine if you thrive in a team environment or prefer less interaction with others.

- How fast-paced of a work environment do you prefer? Some jobs require quick turnarounds and tight deadlines, while others have more flexibility. Decide if you prefer the challenges of a dynamic, high-pressure job or a more steady-state position.

- How much responsibility are you interested in taking on? Entry-level jobs typically have less responsibility, while more senior roles have greater accountability. Assess if you're looking to take on leadership of key initiatives or want to start with a lower level of responsibility.

By evaluating what you want in a job—from the types of tasks and level of challenge to the work environment and amount of responsibility—you can determine good job fits to target. The closer a position matches what will keep you motivated and productive, the happier and more fulfilled you'll be in your work. Finding the right job fit may take time, but by reflecting on what's most important to you in your day-to-day work life, you'll land in the right place.

Finding the Right Job Fit FAQs: Answering Common Questions

Finding the right job fit means determining what really

matters to you in a role and company culture. Here are some common questions to ask yourself:

What are my must-haves?

Think about the - requirements, responsibilities, environment, colleagues, culture - that would make a job satisfying and engaging for you. These could include:

- Flexible work hours

- Opportunities for growth

- Strong company mission I believe in

- Collaborative team environment

Consider what is non-negotiable for your happiness and success. Don't compromise on these must-haves.

What are my "nice-to-haves"?

While not absolutely mandatory, these attributes would make a role even more appealing. Possibly:

- Competitive pay and benefits

- Innovative company

- Ability to work remotely some days

Weigh these nice-to-haves to determine which matter most and how they might tip the scales for one opportunity over another.

What work environment will I thrive in?

Some options include:

- A small start-up with a fast pace

- An established organization with strong structure

- A mid-size company where you can make an impact

Consider whether you prefer highly collaborative or more independent work. Think about the kind of leadership and access you want. The environment and culture should align with your work style and values.

What transferable skills do I have?

Your skills, talents, and experience can apply to various jobs and companies. Identify what you have to offer, such as:

- Communication -Critical thinking
- Project management -Adaptability
- Creativity -Problem-solving

With an understanding of your must-haves, nice-to-haves, ideal work environment, and transferable skills, you'll find job opportunities that fit like a glove. The right role for you is out there—you just have to determine what it looks like so you can go after it with confidence.

Conclusion

So now you stand on the brink of a new opportunity. Armed with clarity of purpose and an understanding of what truly motivates and fulfills you, you're ready to find work that resonates. The search begins within, getting clear on your non-negotiables - the must-haves in a new role. From there, cast a wide net, exploring options that spark your interest. Don't get bogged down in rigid requirements or what looks good on paper. Follow your instincts and look for that feeling of excitement and natural momentum. The right opportunity is out there, waiting to be found. Stay true to yourself, keep an open heart and mind, and it will come. The job that fits like a glove, inspiring your best work. You've got this. Now go get it.

7 How to Ace Any Job Interview

The interview is make or break, and you only have one shot to impress. The good news is, with the right preparation, you've got this. You know your skills and experience are a perfect match, now you just need to convince the interviewer.

Picture yourself walking into that room, full of confidence and charisma. You make eye contact, flash a warm smile, and deliver a firm handshake. As you start talking about your relevant experience, your passion for the work shines through. You have thoughtful questions that show your enthusiasm and interest in the role. By the end of the conversation, the interviewer is envisioning you thriving in the position. You walk out knowing you nailed it. That job is as good as yours.

All you need is the preparation and practice to ace any interview. This guide will give you the tools and techniques to make an amazing first impression and land the job of your dreams. You've got the skills, now get ready to wow them. The interview won't know what hit them.

Preparing for the Interview

To ace any interview, preparation is key. Do your research about the company and role so you can speak knowledgeably about why you're interested in the position and company.

Review the job listing and highlight key qualifications and responsibilities. Then, identify relevant experiences, skills, and strengths you have that match what the company is looking for. Be ready to provide concrete examples to demonstrate them.

Polish your resume to align with the job requirements. Know it inside and out in case they ask you to walk through it.

Practice your answers to common interview questions. Some possibilities:

- Tell me about yourself and your background. Discuss your experience, qualifications, and career goals.

- Why are you interested in this role and company? Express your passion for the work and company mission.

- What are your strengths? How would your coworkers describe you? Discuss 3-4 strengths with examples.

- Why should we hire you? Explain how you are the best candidate for the role based on your relevant experience, skills, work ethic, and enthusiasm for the work.

- Where do you see yourself in five years? Discuss your ambition for career growth while conveying your desire to remain with the company long-term.

Prepare a list of thoughtful questions that show your enthusiasm and interest in the role, team, goals, challenges, etc. Ask about next steps in the process and when you can expect to hear back.

With diligent preparation, you will exude confidence and professionalism. You will be able to have an engaging discussion with your interviewer, demonstrating why you would be a perfect fit.

Researching the Company and Role

To nail that interview, you need to go in armed with knowledge. Do your homework and research both the company and the specific role.

The Company

Check out the company's website to learn about their mission, vision, and values. See what major products or services they offer. Look for recent news articles about the company to get insight into their culture and what they prioritize. The more you understand the company's identity and goals, the better you can demonstrate how you're an ideal fit.

The Role

Carefully read the job listing to understand what skills and experience they're looking for. Then search for similar roles on career sites like Indeed or Monster to determine the typical salary range and day-to-day responsibilities. You might find some useful questions to ask your interviewer.

See if you can find profiles of people currently in that position at the company on LinkedIn. Reach out and ask if they'd be open to a quick phone call to discuss the realities of the role. People often love to help, and you'll get invaluable insider information.

With research, you'll gain confidence from being well-informed. You'll stand out as someone who takes the initiative to really understand the opportunity. And you'll be ready with intelligent questions that show your enthusiasm and passion for the work.

The time you invest will pay off. You'll walk into that interview poised, prepared, and poised to impress. And that dream job will be within your grasp.

Practicing Your Answers to Common Interview Questions

To ace any interview, practice and preparation are key. You need to be ready to answer common interview questions confidently and concisely. Here are some tips to practice:

Do your research.

Learn as much as you can about the company and role so you can speak knowledgeably about why you're interested in the position and company. Study the job listing and company website to get a sense of their mission and values. Come prepared with a few questions that show your enthusiasm and interest in the work.

Review your resume.

Be ready to provide specific examples and stories to illustrate your relevant experience, skills, and career achievements. Your resume will likely be the basis for many of the interview questions, so make sure you know it inside and out.

Anticipate questions and practice your answers.

Some examples include:

- Tell me about yourself and your background. Focus on your experience, qualifications, and career goals that are relevant for this role.

- What are your strengths? Provide concrete examples of your key strengths that will benefit the company. Mention soft skills and technical abilities.

- Why are you leaving your current job? Explain that you're looking for new challenges and career growth, not because you're unhappy in your current role. Focus the conversation on this new opportunity.

- Why do you want this position? Express your genuine enthusiasm for the work, company mission, career growth potential, etc. Back up your answers with specific details.

- Why should we hire you? Explain that you're the best candidate for the role based on your relevant experience, skills, work ethic, and career goals. Provide examples to illustrate your strengths.

With practice, answering interview questions will become second nature. Be authentic in your responses, maintain eye contact, smile, and convey enthusiasm.

Dressing for Interview Success

You've made it to the interview—congratulations! Now it's time to make a stellar first impression. How you dress and present yourself speaks volumes about your professionalism and enthusiasm for the role. Follow these tips to nail your interview attire.

Choose business professional

For most interviews, it's best to dress in business professional or business casual attire. That means:

- Slacks or a knee-length skirt in solid, dark colors like black, navy or gray. Avoid anything too casual like jeans or shorts.

- A button-down shirt, blouse or jacket in a solid color or simple pattern. Make sure anything you wear is clean and wrinkle-free.

- Minimal accessories and jewelry. Keep your look simple and avoid anything too flashy that could distract from what you're saying.

- Polished, professional shoes with a moderate heel. Both ballet flats and stilettos should be avoided.

- Well-groomed hair and minimal fragrances. You want the focus to be on your experience and qualifications, not your appearance or smell.

Do a final check

Before walking into your interview, do a final check to make sure:

- Your clothes are clean and wrinkle-free. Iron or steam anything that needs it.

- You don't have any lint, tags, or loose threads showing.

- Your accessories are minimal and professional.

- Your grooming and hygiene are impeccable. That includes clean and trimmed fingernails, fresh breath, and minimal fragrances.

- You have copies of your resume, a notepad and pen.

- You know the location, have directions and have allotted extra time in case of traffic or parking issues.

Make a memorable entrance

When you arrive, walk in with confidence. Smile, make eye contact, extend a firm handshake, and greet your interviewer by name if known. Your professional and enthusiastic entrance will make a great first impression and set the right tone for an amazing interview.

Arriving Early and Other Interview Day Tips

Arriving early to your interview is one of the best ways to make a good first impression. Aim for 10-15 minutes early so you have time to get settled and review your notes. Take a few deep breaths to help calm any nerves.

Check-in and Meet the Receptionist

Politely introduce yourself to the receptionist and let them know you're there for an interview with [interviewer name]. Their impression of you matters too, so smile, make eye contact, and be courteous. Ask for directions to the interview location if needed.

Do a Quick Self Check

Visit the restroom to make sure you look professional. Check that your clothes are wrinkle-free, collar is straight, and you have nothing in your teeth. For women, check your hair and makeup. For men, check your hair is combed and face is clean-shaven. Freshen up with a mint or piece of gum.

Review Your Notes

While waiting, review the information about the role, team, company, your resume, and experience. Prepare some examples of your relevant accomplishments and how they will benefit the company. Review typical interview questions and your responses. This will boost your confidence for the actual interview.

Make Small Talk

When the interviewer greets you, smile, make eye contact, and offer a firm handshake while saying "It's a pleasure to meet you." Engage in some light chit chat to break the ice before the formal interview begins. Discuss the weather or traffic to start, but avoid controversial topics. Keep things positive and friendly.

Ask Good Questions

Come prepared with some thoughtful questions that show your enthusiasm and interest in the role, team, company, growth opportunities, etc. However, avoid questions about salary, benefits, vacation time, or work hours until an offer has been made. Save those types of questions for a follow-up conversation.

Following these helpful tips will ensure you make an excellent first impression and help calm your nerves before the interview even starts. By arriving early, checking-in confidently, reviewing your notes, and making friendly small talk, you'll go into the actual interview feeling focused and ready to share why you're the perfect candidate for the job.

Using Strong Body Language and Communication Skills

Strong communication and confident body language are key to acing any interview.

Make Eye Contact

Maintaining eye contact shows you are engaged and interested. Look at the interviewer directly when speaking to appear self-assured. If there is more than one interviewer, make eye contact with each person as you speak to them. Don't stare intensely, but do make friendly eye contact, especially when listening to or answering a question. Glancing away occasionally is fine, but avoid looking down or away for long periods, as this can seem disinterested or insecure.

Have an Engaging Smile

Smiling demonstrates positivity, warmth, and enthusiasm. Smile when you first meet the interviewer, when discussing an area of passion or interest, and when the conversation feels more casual. A natural smile can help you appear more likable and charismatic. However, don't keep an overeager smile plastered on your face throughout the entire interview, as this may come across as insincere or nervous. Find the right balance of smiling and serious, engaged listening.

Sit Up Straight and Lean In

Sitting up straight with your shoulders back projects confidence and professionalism. If sitting in a chair, lean forward slightly to appear fully engaged. Crossed legs or arms can seem closed off, so keep your limbs uncrossed when possible. Movement like nodding, hand gestures and shifting your seat forward helps illustrate your passion and interest in the conversation. But avoid fidgeting, foot tapping or other nervous habits.

Speak Clearly and with Confidence

Having well-developed communication abilities is essential for any role. Answer questions succinctly but thoroughly, using a friendly and professional tone. It is fine to show enthusiasm when discussing your relevant experience, interests, and goals. But do not ramble or speak too quickly, as this can be off-putting. Pause if needed to collect your thoughts before responding. Your ability to hold a meaningful dialog with the interviewer is a chance to showcase your verbal communication skills, a highly valued soft skill.

Using these techniques to exhibit strong, positive body language and communication will help ensure you make a great impression.

Asking Thoughtful Questions to the Interviewer

The interview process is a two-way street. While the interviewer is determining if you're the right candidate for the job, you need to assess if the position and company culture are the right fit for you. Asking thoughtful questions shows your enthusiasm and interest in the role, and it gives you valuable insight into the job and company.

Do your research

Before the interview, research the company and role thoroughly. Review the company's website, social media, and recent news reports to get a sense of their products, mission, culture, and current events. The more you know, the better questions you can ask.

Questions about the role

Ask questions that demonstrate your understanding of the key responsibilities and requirements of the position. For example:

- What are the day-to-day responsibilities of this role?

- What are the most important objectives in the first 3 to 6 months?

- What qualities and attributes does the ideal candidate for this position have?

- What programs or software would I need to learn or become proficient in?

Questions about the team and company

Inquire about the team you'd be working with and how the company operates. For example:

1. Can you describe the culture of the department or team I would be joining?

2. What do you like most about working for the company?

3. How would you describe the company's vision and mission?

4. What opportunities does the company provide for career growth and progression?

Closing questions

End by reaffirming your interest and enthusiasm for the role. For example:

- Based on our conversation, what would be the next steps in the interview process?

- Is there any other information about the role or company that would be useful for me to know?

- I'm very enthusiastic about this opportunity. When can I expect to hear from you about next steps?

Asking thoughtful, well-researched questions demonstrates your passion and interest in the company and role. Make sure to listen carefully to the interviewer's responses—the answers could help determine if the job is the right next step in your career.

Following Up After the Interview

Once the interview is over, your work isn't done. Following up appropriately after an interview can make a great impression and help set you apart as a strong candidate. Here are some key tips for following up:

Within 24 hours of your interview, send a thank you email to your interviewer(s). Express your continued interest in and enthusiasm for the role. Reiterate why you're a great fit for the position and company. Mention one or two of the discussion points from your interview to show you were engaged and listening. Keep this email concise while being personable and professional.

A handwritten thank you card is an extra special touch if you have the interviewer's mailing address. Reiterate some of the key points from your thank you email for a double dose of gratitude and enthusiasm. Mail the card within 48 hours of your interview for the best effect.

Connect on LinkedIn. Once you've sent your thank you email, send a request to connect with your interviewer(s) on LinkedIn. In the request, mention your recent interview and reiterate your interest in the role and company. Connecting on LinkedIn, especially if accepted, continues to strengthen your relationship and visibility with the organization.

Follow up on the timeline. If the interviewer indicated when you could expect to hear about next steps or a final decision, follow up if you haven't heard from them by the date specified. Your follow up email should again express your interest and enthusiasm for the role. Check if there are any updates on the hiring timeline or if they need any additional information from you to help move the process along. Provide your availability and flexibility to meet again if needed.

Continuing to express interest and build rapport with your interviewer, especially if done promptly and professionally, can help influence the final hiring decision in your favor.

With the right follow up, you'll ace the interview process from start to finish.

Acing the Interview Process FAQs: Your Top Questions Answered

Interviewing for a new job can be nerve-wracking. You have so many questions running through your mind: What will they ask me? How should I prepare? What should I wear? Take a deep breath—we've got you covered. Here are the answers to your top interview FAQs:

What questions will the interviewer ask me?

Expect a mix of typical interview questions like:

- Tell me about yourself and your work experience.

- Why are you interested in this role and company?

- What are your strengths? Weaknesses?

- Why should we hire you?

- Where do you see yourself in five years?

They may also ask role-specific questions to assess your qualifications. Review the job listing and your resume to prepare examples that highlight relevant experience, skills, and accomplishments.

How should I prepare for the interview?

Do your homework. Learn about the company, their mission and values, products or services, and key people. Check the interviewer's LinkedIn profile. Prepare questions to ask them about the role, team, company goals, etc. to demonstrate your enthusiasm and interest.

Practice your answers to common interview questions. Ask a friend or family member to conduct a mock interview. Hearing yourself speak will help build confidence and smooth out any rough spots.

Review your resume so you can speak to any item on it with clarity and passion. Be ready to provide specific examples and stories to illustrate your key points.

Dress professionally, smile, make eye contact, and give a firm handshake. Your body language and enthusiasm matter.

Bring copies of your resume, a notepad and pen, bottled water, gum or mints, tissues, and anything else that will help you feel comfortable and focused.

What should I wear?

Dress in professional business attire: slacks or a knee-length skirt, button-down shirt, and possibly a blazer. For men, wear slacks, a button-down shirt, and possibly a tie or suit. It is better to be overdressed than underdressed, so if you have any doubts, opt for more formal wear. You want to make a great first impression, so choose clean and pressed clothing in conservative colors. It is always a safe bet to check the company's dress code policy on their website for guidance.

You've prepared thoroughly for your interview, now it's time to go in there and show them what you've got. Walk into that room with confidence, make eye contact, flash a genuine smile. As the conversation begins, speak clearly and passionately about your experience and goals. Ask thoughtful questions that show your enthusiasm and interest in the work. Be authentic in your answers while highlighting your relevant strengths.

Once the interview concludes, maintain your confidence. You've demonstrated the skills and spirit that would make you an invaluable asset to any team. Though the waiting period can be difficult, stay optimistic. If it's meant to be, the offer will come. And if not, you've gained invaluable experience to help ace the next one.

8 Ways to Make Extra Money

There are ways to generate income even when times are tough. You have more skills and talents than you realize, and the gig economy is booming. Whether it's driving for a rideshare service in your spare time, renting out a spare room in your home, or launching a side hustle selling items online, opportunities abound if you look for them. Stay positive, get creative, and keep your head up. The job may have left you, but your ability to earn a living is still within your control. There are always paths forward, even in the face of setbacks. You've got this.

Assess Your Skills and Resources

You've been given an opportunity, so seize it. Take stock of your talents and resources to find ways to generate income on your own terms.

Skills

What are you good at? Make a list of your skills, expertise, and strengths. Think broadly - everything from technical abilities to soft skills like communication or problem-solving. Identify ways to monetize them, whether through freelancing, consulting, teaching, or creating resources to sell.

Network

Reach out to your network and let them know you're

available for freelance or project work. Post on LinkedIn, Facebook groups, and industry forums. Someone in your network may know of work or be able to make introductions.

Develop a product

Do you have knowledge or skills that would translate into an online course, ebook, video tutorial, or other product? Creating and selling your own resources is a great way to generate ongoing passive income.

Drive for a ridesharing service

If you have a reliable vehicle, consider driving for Uber, Lyft, or another ridesharing service in your spare time. You can make decent money, set your own schedule, and get tips from passengers.

Do market research studies

Companies frequently hire people to test products, websites, mobile apps, and more. Look for market research studies in your area on Craigslist, Facebook Marketplace, and NextDoor. Studies typically pay $30 to $500 each depending on the complexity.

Walk dogs

If you're an animal lover, consider starting your own dog walking business. Create a profile on sites like Rover.com, WagWalking.com, and BarklyPets.com. You can make $10 to $20 per walk and walk multiple dogs at once.

Sell unwanted items

Go through your home and look for valuable items you no longer need like designer clothes, collectibles, musical instruments, tools, and recreational equipment. Sell them on eBay, Craigslist, Facebook Marketplace, and NextDoor. Price items competitively and be open to offers.

Sign Up for Gig Economy Apps Like Uber or Instacart

When you've lost your job, making ends meet can be tough. Signing up for gig economy apps is an easy way to generate some extra income on a flexible schedule.

Drive for Uber or Lyft

If you have a reliable car, consider driving for Uber or Lyft in your spare time. You can make $10-15 an hour after accounting for gas and other expenses. The more you drive, the more you'll make. Promo codes and referral bonuses can increase your earnings.

Deliver for Instacart or Postmates

If driving people isn't your thing, you can deliver groceries and takeout for Instacart or Postmates. Shoppers make an average of $10-15 an hour. You'll get paid weekly and can work whenever you want.

Do Tasks on TaskRabbit

TaskRabbit lets you sign up for tasks like delivering packages, helping people move, cleaning houses, and more.

Tasks pay $15-25 an hour on average. You set your own schedule and rates. Build up reviews to get hired more often.

Walk Dogs on Wag or Rover

If you're an animal lover, consider walking dogs in your neighborhood through Wag or Rover. Dog walkers typically make $10-20 for a 30-minute walk. You can walk multiple dogs at once to increase your earnings. Wag and Rover handle scheduling and payments, so it's easy to get started.

There are many ways to earn extra money when you need it most. Give a few gig economy apps a try and stick with the ones you enjoy. In no time, you'll be generating a steady side income until you land your next full-time role.

Sell Unused Items Online

Selling unwanted items online is an easy way to make some quick cash when you've lost your job. Go through your attic, basement, garage, and storage units and pull out anything you no longer need or want. Then, post the items for sale on websites like eBay, Craigslist, and Facebook Marketplace.

List your items with details and photos

Provide a description of the item's condition, measurements, model number, and any accessories. Post pictures from multiple angles so buyers know exactly what they're getting. The more details the better. Mention any imperfections or signs of wear so you're upfront and honest with buyers.

Price items to sell

Do some research to determine a fair asking price for your items based on the current market value. You may need to adjust prices down for a quick sale. It's better to sell at a lower price than not sell at all. Consider offering free local pickup to avoid shipping costs. You can also run sales and promotions to move items faster.

Respond to interested buyers quickly

Once your items are posted, be proactive in responding to any questions or offers from interested parties. The faster you engage with potential buyers, the more likely you are to actually sell your items. Negotiate the best deal you can and finalize the sale.

Meet for local pickups cautiously

If you offer local pickup, take general safety precautions. Meet buyers in a public place, like a coffee shop. Let someone know where you're going and who you're meeting. Trust your instincts—if something feels off about a buyer, don't complete the sale. Your safety is most important.

Selling unwanted belongings is an simple way to earn extra money when you're between jobs. Clear out the clutter from your home, list your items attractively online, price to sell quickly, and connect with interested buyers right away. Be safe meeting for local pickups and you'll be earning money from your unwanted items in no time.

Rent Out Extra Space in Your Home

One of the easiest ways to generate extra income when

you've lost your job is to rent out unused space in your home. Do you have an extra bedroom, basement, or garage that's just collecting dust? Consider turning that wasted space into money each month.

List your extra room on home-sharing sites like Airbnb, VRBO, and HomeAway. You can charge a nightly or weekly rate and earn money from short-term rentals. Make sure to take appealing photos, set a competitive price, and build your listing to highlight the benefits and amenities. Promote your listing on social media to increase views and bookings.

If you prefer more long-term tenants, you can also list your space on sites like Craigslist, Facebook Marketplace, or rent.com. When screening potential roommates or tenants, ask for references and run a background check to find trustworthy individuals. Charge a monthly rent that is at least 2/3 of the going rate for similar rooms or apartments in your neighborhood.

Do you have a standalone garage, barn, or shed? These buildings also present an opportunity to generate rental income. List the space for storage, parking a vehicle, or hobby work like woodworking or pottery. Add amenities like electricity, temperature control, and 24/7 access to increase what you can charge.

Renting out part of your home is an easy way to earn money on the side, especially if you've recently lost your main source of income. Keep good records for tax purposes, draft a solid lease agreement to protect yourself legally, and maintain the space to keep tenants happy. With some extra effort, that unused area in your home could put hundreds of dollars in your pocket each month.

Take on Freelance Work or Consulting

One of the best ways to earn extra money when you've lost your job is by taking on freelance work or doing consulting in your field of expertise.

Find freelance jobs on websites like Upwork, Fiverr, or Freelancer.

These sites allow you to create a profile to advertise your skills and services. You can then apply for freelance jobs that match your experience. Common types of freelance work include writing, programming, graphic design, virtual assistance, and more. The pay will vary but can be $25-$100 per hour or more for specialized skills.

Offer your services as an independent consultant.

If you have experience in a specific industry or job function, consider consulting. You can help businesses in your area of expertise on a project basis. Market your consulting services through your personal network, LinkedIn, and your own professional website. Charge $50-$200 per hour or more depending on your skills and experience.

Drive for Uber, Lyft or deliver for Uber Eats, Postmates or DoorDash.

Ridesharing and food delivery driving are easy ways to make

decent money on a flexible schedule. You can earn $10-$15 per ride or delivery in many areas. The only requirements are a reliable vehicle, insurance, a clean driving record and a smartphone.

Do market research studies.

Companies frequently hire people to provide opinions and insights into products, services, and topics. You can sign up with market research firms like Survey Junkie, Swagbucks, and InboxDollars to participate in online surveys, focus groups, clinical trials, and taste tests. You typically earn $5-$15 for each study you complete, which you can do from anywhere with an Internet connection.

Rent out a spare room in your home on Airbnb or VRBO.

If you have an extra bedroom, consider renting it out to travelers in your area. You can charge $30-$100 per night or more depending on the location and amenities. While it does require making sure the room is clean and prepared for each guest, it's an easy way to generate money from an asset you already have.

Pick Up Temporary Jobs

Losing your job is tough, but picking up temporary work can help make ends meet while you look for something more permanent. Here are a few options to consider:

Drive for a ridesharing service.

If you have a reliable car, sign up to drive for Uber, Lyft, or a similar service in your area. You can work whenever you want and earn decent money, especially during busy times like evenings and weekends. The flexible schedule also leaves time open for interviews and networking.

Do freelance work.

Websites like Upwork, Fiverr, and Freelancer offer opportunities for freelance work like writing, editing, graphic design, virtual assistance, and more. Build up your profile, apply for jobs that match your skills, and earn money for the projects you complete. Freelancing lets you gain valuable experience and work from anywhere.

Check out temp agencies.

Temporary staffing agencies specialize in placing workers in short-term jobs. Register with a few agencies in your area and let them know the types of positions you're interested in. They'll contact you when jobs that match your skills become available. Temp jobs can be a source of immediate income and may even turn into long-term work.

Drive for a food delivery service.

If you prefer to avoid the customer service aspects of ridesharing, delivering food for services like Uber Eats, Postmates, or DoorDash is an easy way to generate income using your vehicle. You pick up orders from local restaurants and deliver them to customers, earning money for each delivery. The job has a lot of flexibility so you can work whenever and earn good tips.

do odd jobs on the side.

Check websites that offer local odd jobs and taskrabbit positions. Things like helping people move, cleaning houses, delivering groceries, walking dogs, etc. are easy ways to bring in some money without a long-term commitment. Let friends and family know you're available for small tasks as well. Every little bit helps when you're between jobs.

The key is to start generating income from multiple sources as soon as possible. Pick up temporary work that fits your skills and schedule, gain valuable experience, and keep moving forward. With hard work and persistence, this challenging time will pass.

Start a Side Hustle Doing Something You Love

A side hustle is a great way to generate extra income doing something you enjoy. Whether you have a hobby, skill, or interest that could translate into a money-making endeavor, give it a shot. The additional funds will help offset the loss of your primary income stream.

Sell Your Skills

Do you have a talent or skill that others would pay for? Things like photography, graphic design, online tutoring, and freelance writing are all great side hustles. Set up a profile on a freelancing platform like Upwork or Fiverr and start marketing your services. Build up reviews and ratings, set your rates, and you'll be making money in no time.

Turn a Hobby into Cash

We all have hobbies and interests that we're passionate about. Look for ways to monetize your hobby. If you're an avid reader, start a book review blog or podcast. If you love gaming, stream yourself playing on Twitch. Crafty types can sell handmade goods on Etsy. Gardening enthusiasts can sell plants, flowers or produce at a local farmers market. Pursue the activities you enjoy and the money will follow.

Drive for a Rideshare Service

Driving for Uber, Lyft or another rideshare service is an easy way to generate extra money in your spare time. You can work when you want and set your own schedule. All you need is a reliable car, a clean driving record, and a smartphone to get started. The extra money you earn can really add up over time. Many drivers are able to make $500-$1000 per week or more.

Online Surveys and Market Research Studies

Filling out online surveys in your spare time can generate some easy cash. Check sites like Survey Junkie, Swagbucks, and InboxDollars. They offer surveys on a range of topics. While you may only make a few dollars per survey, over time it can add up to a nice chunk of change. Some studies also offer higher payouts for phone or in-person interviews and focus groups.

The key is to find a side hustle you genuinely enjoy and stick with it. With time and consistency, you can turn it into a steady source of income to help you through this difficult period. Don't get discouraged if it takes a while to get off the ground. Many successful businesses today started as someone's side hustle. Stay positive and keep putting in the work. The extra money will come.

Donate Plasma for Cash

Donating plasma is a great way to earn some extra cash when you've lost your job. Plasma donation centers will pay you for your time and the plasma you provide. The plasma you donate is used to create lifesaving medicines for people with rare, chronic diseases. By donating just a few hours of your time each week, you can earn $200 to $400 per month.

To get started, find a plasma donation center near you and check their eligibility requirements. As long as you meet their criteria, which typically includes being in good health, over 18, and over 110 pounds, you're ready to become a donor.

When you first visit a center, you'll go through an initial screening process which includes checking your blood pressure, pulse, temperature, and protein levels. This helps ensure you can safely donate plasma. If all looks good, you can begin donating right away.

The actual plasma donation process, known as plasmapheresis, uses a machine to draw blood, separate the plasma, and return your red blood cells to you. It usually takes between 1 to 3 hours for your first visit, then around 45 minutes to 2 hours for subsequent donations. You can donate plasma up to twice a week.

The plasma you provide during each donation can be used to create 20 or more doses of plasma-derived therapies. By donating regularly, you're making a life-changing impact on patients in need. And of course, you'll earn money for each successful donation. Most centers pay with prepaid debit cards, direct deposit, or PayPal so you have quick access to your funds.

Donating plasma is a simple way to earn extra money when times are tough. You're providing a valuable resource to help save lives, all while earning hundreds of dollars per month. If you've recently lost your job or source of income, donating plasma could be a good option to generate some quick cash flow during your transition.

FAQ: Answering Common Questions on Making Money When Laid Off

The bills aren't going to stop coming in just because you lost your job. While searching for new work, here are some ways to generate extra income to help make ends meet.

Drive for a ridesharing service.

If you have a reliable car, consider signing up to drive for Uber, Lyft, or a similar service. You can work whenever you want and earn decent money, especially on weekends and evenings. The more you drive, the more you make. This is an easy way to generate quick cash flow.

Do freelance work.

Websites like Upwork, Fiverr, and 99Designs are filled with freelance jobs in areas like writing, graphic design, online tutoring, and more. Find jobs that match your skills and interests. Freelancing allows you to work from home on your own schedule. While pay varies, even earning $20-30/hour for 10-15 hours a week can provide a good income boost.

Sell unwanted items.

Go through your attic, basement, garage, and closets and pull out anything you no longer need to sell online or at a yard sale. You can sell clothing, books, toys, furniture, decor, and electronics on sites like eBay, Craigslist, Facebook Marketplace or at a local consignment shop. Price items reasonably and be open to offers. Any money you earn from decluttering your space is money you didn't have before.

Do market research studies.

Companies often hire people to provide opinions and insights on new products, services, and ideas. Sign up with a market research firm like Survey Junkie, Swagbucks, or InboxDollars to complete online surveys and focus groups. While you won't get rich, you can earn $5 to $25 per study. Do a few a week and it adds up to $50-$200/month.

Answer common questions.

Websites like JustAnswer and Chegg Tutors pay people to provide answers to commonly asked questions on a wide range of topics. If you have expertise in areas like tech support, teaching, medical, legal, or business, you can sign up to answer questions. Pay varies but can average $20-$50 per answer. The more questions you answer, the more you earn.

uncertain, stay determined. Stay creative. Stay flexible. New paths will emerge as you push forward each day. Hard times often lead to greater things, so keep your head high. There are always possibilities if you look for them.

9 How to Switch Careers When You Have No Relevant Experience

Changing careers seems impossible when you have no relevant experience. But with the right mindset and strategies, you can successfully switch paths, even when facing obstacles like outdated skills, lack of connections, and confidence gaps. Stop viewing your situation as an insurmountable challenge. See it as an opportunity to forge a new, more fulfilling professional identity. With hard work and persistence, you can overcome perceived barriers, learn new skills, and land a job in an area you feel passionate about.

The road ahead won't be easy, but by tapping into your grit and growth mindset, you can transition into a new career and build experience from the ground up. It's time to rewrite your professional story.

Assess Your Interests and Values

The first step is to determine what really drives you in your career and life. Think about the work activities, causes, and impact that motivate you. What gets you excited and passionate? Maybe it's creating something new, helping others, solving complex problems, or working with your hands. Don't limit yourself to your current field - explore what else is out there.

Once you've identified potential areas of interest, evaluate your key values and priorities. Things like work-life balance, growth opportunities, company culture, and compensation. Determine what is most important to you right now. For example, if work-life balance and job stability are top concerns after a layoff, you may want to consider fields with strong growth that offer flexibility and security.

- Brainstorm a list of fields, jobs or companies that align with your key interests and values. Do some research on the qualifications, responsibilities, and typical career paths in each area. Look for roles that leverage your transferable skills and experience.

- See if you can gain any exposure to appealing new fields through volunteering, internships, job shadowing or online courses. Start building your experience and connections in new areas of interest. Expanding your network is key.

- Don't feel limited by a lack of direct experience. Many of your skills - communication, critical thinking, work ethic - translate across fields. Focus on your related strengths, motivation for the work, and ability to learn. With the right mindset, you can pivot into a new career path.

The process of changing careers when you have limited experience takes dedication. But by identifying your passions, priorities, and transferable skills - and taking action to gain valuable exposure in new areas - you put yourself in the best position to land in a role and field of work that motivates and fulfills you.

Identify Transferable Skills from Past Jobs

You may feel like you have no experience for a new career, but that's not true. Transferable skills from past jobs can help you switch careers.

Identify Broad Skills

Think about broad skills you've gained, like:

- Communication: Have you explained complex ideas to others? Dealt with upset clients? These skills transfer across fields.

- Problem-solving: Solving issues, troubleshooting systems, and finding solutions apply to many jobs.

- Time management: Meeting deadlines, efficiency, and organization are useful everywhere.

- Creativity: Coming up with new ideas, approaches, or solutions shows you can think outside the box.

Analyze Your Experience

Dig into your work history. What did you do day-to-day? Notice subtle skills you gained, e.g.:

- Research and analysis: Did you gather and evaluate information to make recommendations? Useful for many careers.

- Adaptability: Have you adjusted to changes, learned new systems, or taken on more responsibility?

Adaptability is a must for career switchers.

- Leadership: Even if you weren't a manager, did you mentor others, delegate work, or make team contributions? Leadership ability transfers well.

Don't discount experience that seems unrelated. Soft skills from any field, customer service roles, freelance work, volunteering, and hobbies can all apply to a new career. The more you can demonstrate transferable skills from your background, the more attractive you'll be to potential employers, even without direct experience.

Research Growth Industries and in-Demand Jobs

The job market is always evolving, and entire industries can change dramatically over time. Many jobs that were commonplace just a decade or two ago have been replaced by automation and technology. However, with change comes opportunity. New, fast-growing fields are emerging, and jobs that leverage human skills like critical thinking, complex problem-solving, and social/emotional intelligence are on the rise.

To find a career that will be in-demand for years to come, do some research on growth industries and jobs. Some areas poised for major growth include:

- Healthcare. As the population ages, healthcare is expanding rapidly. Everything from nurses and home health aides to medical assistants and physical therapists are in high demand. These jobs provide meaningful work helping others in a growing industry.

- Renewable Energy. The renewable energy sector is taking off, with solar and wind power at the forefront. Jobs like solar installers, wind turbine technicians, and sustainability specialists are in demand. This field is a great option if you want to work in an industry that is good for the environment.

- Technology. While some tech jobs are at risk of automation, others leverage skills that artificial intelligence struggles with. User experience designers, data scientists, software engineers, and IT security specialists are all fast-growing, well-paying jobs. These roles require both technical and human skills that won't easily be replaced by machines.

- Business Services. Areas like human resources, marketing, project management, and finance are essential for businesses. Jobs such as HR specialists, digital marketers, project managers, and financial analysts are growing quickly. These roles provide opportunities across industries.

The key is to identify fields that play to your strengths, then explore jobs within those areas that you find interesting and impactful. Do informational interviews, job shadow, or take a course to learn more. With proactive research and preparation, you can develop skills and experience for an in-demand career, even without direct experience. The future is bright—you just have to find the right path to get there.

Consider Getting Additional Education or Training

Going back to school or pursuing additional training is one method for gaining relevant experience in a new field.

Enroll in a certification or degree program

If you want a career change but lack experience, formal education is a great place to start. Enrolling in a certification, associate's degree, or bachelor's degree program related to your target career can provide you with essential knowledge and skills to land an entry-level job.

Coursework exposes you to key concepts and best practices in the field. You'll build a foundation of expertise to draw from in interviews and on the job. Many programs also include internships or work-study opportunities, allowing you to gain real-world experience.

Don't have time for a full degree? Consider a certificate or certification. Many careers offer specialized credentials to demonstrate your competence. For example, project management certificates for aspiring PMs or medical coding certifications for healthcare. These focused programs typically take less time but still carry weight with employers.

Pursue online or in-person training

If formal education isn't the right path, look into targeted job training programs. Many are offered online via platforms like Coursera, Udacity or Udemy, allowing you to learn on your own schedule. Subjects range from coding and web development to digital marketing and data analysis.

In-person trainings are also an option. Check with local career centers, community colleges or private institutions for short courses or boot camps in your area of interest. While less structured than a degree program, these trainings expose you to in-demand skills and often lead to certifications that validate your new abilities.

Continuous learning is key for any successful career change. Additional education and training allow you to build knowledge and experience from the ground up. With hard work and persistence, you can pivot into a new role, even without direct experience. The investment in developing relevant skills and expertise will pay off in finding fulfilling work you're qualified to do.

Look for Entry-Level or Temporary Positions

Looking for entry-level or temporary positions in your new field is a great way to get your foot in the door, even without direct experience. These roles often have lower barriers to entry, allowing you to pivot into a new career.

Apply for internships or apprenticeships

Internships and apprenticeships provide valuable on-the-job experience. Though often unpaid, they allow you to learn skills and make professional connections. Look for internships at smaller companies where you'll get more hands-on experience. Be willing to start at the bottom to work your way up.

Consider freelancing or contract work

Freelancing, consulting, or contract work in your desired field allows you to gain relevant experience while earning income. You may be able to find freelance work through websites like Upwork, Fiverr, or Freelancer. Build your portfolio by taking on small jobs at first. Look for contract roles through staffing agencies that place candidates in temporary positions. Be open to short-term jobs to start building experience and networking.

Apply to entry-level roles

Don't be afraid to apply for entry-level jobs in your target career, even if you lack direct experience. Emphasize transferable skills from other jobs or areas of your life. Explain your passion for the work and desire to transition into the field. You may need to start in a more junior role, but you can quickly advance as you gain on-the-job experience.

Consider going back to school

Additional education or training is a great way to pivot into a new career, especially if you need to develop technical skills. Explore programs at local colleges, boot camps, or online courses to strengthen your knowledge and resume. Look for programs that offer internships or lead to certifications that will make you a strong candidate for jobs.

With determination, an openness to learn, and a willingness to start small, you can successfully change careers even without direct experience. Entry-level roles, temporary work, further education, and internships are all avenues to gain the necessary experience to advance in your new field. Stay patient and keep putting one foot in front of the other.

Highlight Relevant Experience on Your Resume

When changing careers, your resume is your first impression. Highlighting relevant experience shows how you're a great fit for the new role, even without direct experience.

Focus on Transferable Skills

Transferable skills like communication, critical thinking, and problem-solving are useful across jobs. Review the job listing for required skills and emphasize related examples from your work history. For example, if the new role requires project management, discuss how you've organized and executed key initiatives in previous positions.

Use active verbs like "facilitated," "spearheaded," or "optimized" to strengthen your relevant experience. Discuss how you can hit the ground running with your transferable skills.

Emphasize Relevant Qualifications

Do you have related education, certifications, or credentials? Highlight them prominently on your resume. For example, if you're moving into healthcare from another field, feature medical assisting or nursing degrees up top.

Relevant coursework, workshops, and continuing education also demonstrate your commitment to the new career path.

Discuss how these qualifications will allow you to excel in the new role.

Focus on Related Roles and Responsibilities

Look for parallels between your current and target roles. If moving into project management from customer service, for example, emphasize responsibilities like collaborating cross-functionally, streamlining processes, and resolving issues. Discuss how these related experiences will help you succeed in the new position.

Consider Temporary Positions or Side Gigs

Temporary positions, internships, shadowing, and side gigs in your target career provide valuable experience. Look for short-term opportunities to build your resume and connections in the field. Be open about your career change goals and desire to gain relevant experience.

With strategic resume tailoring, you can overcome lack of direct experience. Focus on your transferable skills, relevant qualifications, related roles, and temporary positions in your target career. Discuss how these prepare you to hit the ground running in a new position. With the right pitch, you'll convince employers to take a chance on you.

Network and Use Connections to Find Opportunities

When you find yourself out of work without the skills or experience for your desired new career, networking and leveraging your connections is key.

Reach out to your network

Contact people in your network who currently have the kind of job you want. Ask them out for coffee or a quick phone call to learn more about their role and company. Let them know you're interested in switching careers and see if they have any advice or know of any opportunities. They may be able to refer you to others in the field or even help you land an interview.

Use LinkedIn to connect

LinkedIn is a great tool for networking and staying up to date with connections in your desired industry. Join relevant LinkedIn groups to connect with others, post questions, and look for job leads. Also, check profiles of people in roles you aspire to. See what kind of experience and education they have. You may find new connections or get ideas for skills or certifications to develop.

Attend industry events

Look for local events, conferences, and meetups in your target industry or job function. This is a chance to make valuable face-to-face connections, learn more about the field, and uncover new opportunities. Go with the intention of listening, asking questions, and building new relationships. Share your goal of switching careers—you never know who may be able to help or pass along your resume.

Consider temporary or part-time work

Taking a temporary, contract or part-time role in your

desired field can be a great way to gain valuable experience. Look for short-term jobs or projects that could expose you to the work, culture, and key skills. Be upfront that you're looking to switch careers. If it's a good fit, it may even turn into a permanent role. At a minimum, you'll walk away with new experience and connections to help in your job search.

The key is putting in the effort to build relationships and look for ways to get on-the-job experience. While the work may be outside your comfort zone, networking and creative opportunities can lead to a new career, even without the matching background. With determination, you can make a switch to a fulfilling new role.

Consider Volunteering to Gain Experience

Volunteering is one of the best ways to gain valuable experience for a new career, especially when you lack the specific skills or background that most employers are looking for.

Find opportunities in your target field

Seek out volunteer roles that expose you to the type of work you want to do. If you want to become a teacher, volunteer at a local school. If you're interested in nursing, volunteer at a hospital or clinic. This hands-on experience will give you insight into the day-to-day responsibilities of that career and help you determine if it's the right path for you.

Make valuable connections

Volunteering allows you to network and connect with others

in your desired field. The people you meet may be able to offer guidance, mentoring, or even job leads to help launch your new career. Don't be afraid to let people know your goals and ask questions about their work. Building allies and champions can be instrumental to making a career switch.

Develop and strengthen skills

Take on volunteer work that allows you to utilize and improve skills that will be relevant for your new career. If you need to boost your technical skills, look for opportunities to do online training or take free courses on sites like Coursera or Udemy in your spare time. The more you practice, the more confident and capable you'll feel in your new role.

Ask for references

Once you've established yourself as a reliable and valuable volunteer, ask supervisors or colleagues if they would be willing to provide a reference for you. Having references that can speak to your abilities and work ethic in a professional capacity will strengthen your applications for new job opportunities.

With time and persistence, volunteering in your desired field can open up doors to help launch your new career. The experience, connections, skills, and references you gain will make you a standout candidate, even without traditional experience.

Stay Positive and Persistent When Job Hunting

Staying positive and persistent is key when job hunting, especially if you lack directly relevant experience. It can be easy to get discouraged but maintain an optimistic mindset. Some tips to help you push through:

Focus on Transferable Skills

You have more to offer than you realize. Identify soft skills and transferable experience that apply to your new field. For example, customer service, communication, problem-solving, and management abilities are useful across many roles. Emphasize how these adaptable talents will benefit the new position.

Network

Connecting with others in your desired industry can uncover hidden opportunities and open doors. Reach out to former colleagues, mentors, and people currently in that field. Let them know you're on the market and ask for informational interviews. Build genuine relationships - you never know where connections may lead.

Consider Temporary or Volunteer Work

Gaining experience, even if unpaid, allows you to strengthen your resume, learn new skills, and get your foot in the door. Look for temporary assignments, internships, or volunteer work in your target area. Be willing to start small to work your way up as you prove yourself. Some experience is better than none.

Keep Applying

Persistence and repetition are key. Keep actively searching and applying for new roles that match your goals. It can take time for the right opportunity to appear. Stay up-to-date with the latest job listings and be ready to submit applications on short notice. While waiting to hear back from applications, work on your resume, online profiles, and interview skills.

Don't Get Discouraged

Searching for a new career path when you lack direct experience can be challenging and demoralizing. But staying positive and not giving up is essential. It only takes one opportunity to get you started. Maintain confidence in your abilities and continue moving closer to your goals each day, however small the steps. With hard work and persistence, you will achieve your dream career change.

10 Your Top Questions Answered

What are my rights as an employee?

As an employee, you have certain rights even after termination. This includes compensation for unused paid time off, continued health insurance coverage, and unemployment benefits. Review the details of your termination and employee handbook for specifics. If you feel you were wrongly terminated, you may want to consult with a labor lawyer regarding your legal options.

How long will my severance/unemployment last?

Severance pay, and unemployment benefits provide temporary income after a layoff, but are not meant to be permanent solutions. Use this time wisely to update your resume, build your professional network, and search for a new job. The sooner you start planning your next steps, the better prepared you'll be when your benefits end.

Should I apply for unemployment benefits?

Absolutely, apply for unemployment benefits as soon as possible after being laid off. As an employee, you've paid into the unemployment insurance system, so take advantage of the benefits you're entitled to. The amount you receive will be based on your previous income and the number of dependents you claim. While unemployment, make finding new work your full-time job to avoid relying on benefits long-term.

How can I explain the situation to family and friends?

Losing a job is difficult, and it's normal to feel worried about how others may react. Be open and honest in your communication without shame. Let close ones know you've been laid off, but you have a plan to find new work. Ask for their patience, support, and encouragement during your transition. Surround yourself with positivity to help ease feelings of stress or self-doubt.

What if my family depends on my income?

If you're the sole income earner for your family, being laid off can be an especially scary situation. Speak with your employer, creditors, and service providers right away to request temporary relief, reduced or deferred payments. Apply for additional assistance like food stamps or welfare if needed. Create a bare bones budget, cut unnecessary expenses, and prioritize essential bills to make your remaining funds last. Let creditors know you intend to repay any reduced or deferred amounts as soon as you secure new employment. Staying proactive can help relieve financial hardship during unemployment.

The laid-off life you've left behind is but one chapter in your story. The pages that remain are yours to write. Stay open to new opportunities and adventures that stretch your talents in ways you've yet to imagine. Have faith that purpose, and passion await you, even if you can't yet see where the road may lead. Stay focused on your goals, leverage your skills, and keep putting one foot in front of the other. Don't dwell on what was lost, look toward the opportunities now open to you. You have so much talent, experience, and determination. This is merely a chance to pivot into something new and better!